HOW TO WRITE

A KILLER SAT ESSAY

...IN 25 MINUTES OR LESS!

TOM CLEMENTS

HIT 'EM UP PUBLISHING

CALIFORNIA 2011

TC TUTORING "Join the Charge to Higher Education" www.tctutoring.net / tctutoring@att.net

TC TUTORING
346 Rheem Blvd, Suite 110-B
Moraga, California, 94556
www.tctutoring.net

First Edition: January 2011

Cover design by Namita Kapoor

Printed in the United States of America
ISBN: 978-0-578-07665-2

BLURBS

Joanne Levy-Prewitt, syndicated columnist for the San Francisco Chronicle
WOW! I am so impressed with this book. Talk about distillation. With incredible style and humor, Tom has managed to distill the essence of the SAT essay into 160 very readable pages.

RH, California
Tom's book was a crucial part of my preparation for the SAT. It not only taught me how to write an essay but it also gave me the confidence to do so. I don't know how I could possibly face the SAT essay without this helpful information. In addition, my sister used this material and ended up getting a perfect score on her paper. Tom's book will relieve any fears you have about writing the SAT essay.

KW, California
With Tom's guidelines, content examples, and transition sentences, writing the SAT essay was a breeze. Before even receiving the topic, I already had general supporting evidence sure to fit any prompt and transition and topic sentences for every paragraph. By making the essay into a universal outline where you can mix and match supporting points, Tom has created an ingenious method for writing an excellent essay in a short period of time, without the stress of trying to figure out structural details!

BK, India
I'm a grade 11 student from India and have my SAT next month. While searching for tips on acing the SAT essay, I happened to stumble upon a 2 chapter sample of your book, "How to Write a Killer SAT Essay in 25 Minutes or Less". Barely 2 pages through the first chapter, I found myself thinking, "Haha. This guy is a genius." By the time I reached the end, I was sold.

SH, California
Tom's book has a bunch of really simple strategies that are very applicable to the essay portion of the SAT. Since Tom had already helped me "prefabricate" and outline my essay before I even read the prompt, the first part of the SAT was a real breeze and I made it through without a whole lot of stress. The rest of the SAT test is evil, but Tom's book definitely simplifies the seemingly impossible essay. He's a real lifesaver!

AK, California
This book was my SAT fairy godmother. Reading the previous year's prompts and learning easy ways to develop a quick, concise, and intelligent essay lowered my stress level more than any other preparation could. Thanks to Tom I received a perfect score and blew those Readers away. The wit and wisdom apparent in this helpful guide gave me a healthier perspective on the overall SAT. It's all a game, and Tom will teach you to beat the inside tricks that the SAT essay writers create. Tom uses language that teens can relate to, dissecting the essay and making everything seem much simpler. He's the coolest tutor and writer around. Thanks, Tom!

CW, California
You need to know the system if you're going to beat it, and Tom's book is the best way to do so.

DD, California
Going into the SAT, the part I feared most was the essay. Tom really put me at ease and I was able to apply all of the techniques to my essay. The content examples fit perfectly with any prompt and I feel like I would be prepared to take on any essay topic thrown at me.

JL, California
When it came time to write my 25 minute essay during the SAT, I realized how much of an advantage I had compared to the other students. Prior to even knowing the topic, I was well prepared to put my pen to work the second I was allowed to open my test booklet, and had confidence in the essay I was constructing.

NB, California
I went into my SAT test completely assured that I would receive at least a 10 on my essay with minimal stress. Thanks to Tom's book I was able to do just that. I breezed right through it. (Maybe one day everyone will use the Tom Clements technique and then the College Board would have to revise their test!)

SG, California
I thought it would be nearly impossible to prepare and write a solid essay in 25 minutes until I took Tom's SAT course and read his book about the SAT essay. Reading the book helped me enter the SAT feeling confident and prepared, and I surprised myself by getting a great score of 11. Tom's book is highly recommended. And don't think it's like any other boring SAT textbook, you'll stay interested in it and, in addition, learn a few fun facts that have nothing to do with the SAT!

SC, California
Tom's book blew me away! When I started reading his book, I had no idea how to construct an essay in 25 minutes and I was scared to death of even trying. But he showed us how to structure the essay, add transitions, and prefabricate a lot of the content stuff we needed to support our thesis. His book is awesome! I came away totally prepared for whatever prompt the SAT was going to throw at me. Tom, you're the best.

HM, California
The SAT people are certifiably crazy for making you write an entire essay in 25 minutes. And yet, Tom has found some magical way to make it possible. Not only do his strategies instruct you how to write an essay they want to read and beat the time crunch; most importantly they give you confidence in your ability to ace the test. And when you're sitting in that desk on the day of the SAT, confidence is invaluable!

CONTEXT

Originality is nothing but judicious imitation.
Voltaire

Good artists borrow, great artists steal.
Picasso

I think conscious, deliberate imitation of a piece of prose one admires
can be good training, a means toward finding one's own voice as a
narrative writer.
Ursula Le Guin

Everything I've ever written has bits and pieces of everything I've
ever heard. Any rapper that tells you different is a liar. You can't
write a book if you've never read a book. And if you've read five
books and you try to write a book, your book will mainly encompass
the themes and the context of the five books you've read.
Bun B, rapper, interviewed in The Believer.

All writers stand on the shoulders of other writers. All writers use
unoriginal research. Not all stories arrive pure and complete in the
mind. It's all part of the stew.
Jon Carroll, San Francisco Chronicle columnist

Fact is like clay. You shape it to your own ends.
John Gregory Dunne

Table of Contents

≡

1—White Space

As George Orwell pointed out in Animal Farm: "All animals are created equal, but some animals are more equal than others." So it is with the SAT, nominally composed of nine equal sections, one of which — the essay — is definitely more equal than the others.

Not only is the essay the first section you encounter on the SAT, but you're expected to construct — in a rush — a dazzling piece of prose from scratch on two pages of blank paper. Bummer.

In terms of the sheer terror it evokes among test takers, the essay is easily every high school student's personal nightmare on Elm street. In fact, Freddy Krueger's got nothing on the folks at ETS, the compassion-challenged academics who administer the SAT test for the College Board with the clear intent of messing with your plans for college. And nowhere is that more apparent than in the way they've rigged the essay.

Imagine: you've got 25 minutes to compose — unedited — a masterful, structurally sound, intellectually solid, vocabulary-dense prose piece that shows both your command of language and your understanding of literary, historical and technological trends. Right.

Truth be told, it's a scam from top to bottom. And in this book I'm going to teach you how to scam the scammers. In these pages, I've assembled a collection of real-world tricks and techniques that enable you not only to eliminate the fear and loathing associated with the SAT essay but also to beat the clock, ace the prompt and bag a top score of 11 or 12.

And this isn't just me talking. I've trained hundreds of students to produce high-quality SAT prose under pressure-cooker conditions. In fact, over 30% of the students who have taken my SAT writing courses have received scores of 11 or 12 on their SAT essays. No mean feat.

And, to help show you the way, many of these successful student essays are re-produced here — in full and in part — so that you can take advantage of the insights provided by your peers.

≡
___

I'm a firm believer in teaching-by-doing. And the first step in doing is seeing it done right.

Basketball Jones

Case in point: I became an All-League point guard in high school (which eventually led to a full ride to college) after spending the summer of my sophomore year watching Art Diaz, the star player on our basketball team, snake his way through countless pickup games, leaving most opponents clutching for air as he blew by them on his way to the basket.

Over the summer, I studied his moves, practiced his routines, played alongside him and eventually incorporated his magic into a style I could call my own. Imitation, in other words, is the sincerest form of flattery. Not only that, but imitation is the first step in learning how to develop and perfect your own individual style.

Watching Diaz play, I could see the possibilities for my own game starting to materialize.

Sampling

In the rap world, imitation is called sampling. You know how it works. Ice Cube, Dr. Dre, Eminem, all those street-smart artists find a nice melodic riff to use as a foundation for a new song, then overlay some syncopated beats and real-world lyrics to complete the mix.

Take, for example, "It Was a Good Day", Ice Cube's ironic anthem to street life in South Central LA. The song borrows its melody from the Isley brothers' "Footsteps in the Dark", transforming the tune into a drive-by dreamscape where a good day means "I didn't even have to use my AK."

The fact that Ice Cube reached back a couple of decades to sample an Isley Brothers tune gives rap credence to D. H. Lawrence's famous quote: "The ideas of one generation become the instincts of the next."

People everywhere, in other words, build on the work of those around them and the work of those that went before. That's the way we're going to do it here.

We're going to build a twenty-five minute essay on top of some tried and true American events like Civil Rights and Women's Rights, then we'll mix in some heavy riffs from literature using clips from books like *The Scarlet Letter* and the *Great Gatsby*. To cover all the bases, we might even throw in something from technology like the NASA space shuttle disaster or the famous meltdown of the Russian nuclear reactor at Chernobyl. All this will give you the content you need to write an impressive, detailed essay and *appear* to be an expert in history, literature and technology. Remember, appearances trump reality when it comes to writing the SAT essay.

In the meager 25 minutes you're allotted to write the essay, you need to *appear* to be well-read, culturally sophisticated, historically hip and a master of prose style and structure. Don't worry, I'm going to show you how to do all that — and more — with a minimum of muss and fuss, all within the twenty-five minute time frame.

I'm going to show you, in other words, how to prefabricate a large part of your essay — in terms of content, structure and transitions — so that you can approach judgement day fully armed and ready to rock and roll with whatever essay prompt the SAT folks throw at you.

But first, just so you know what you're getting into, a few words on the general structure of the SAT.

SAT Structure

Like Gaul (ancient France), which Caesar (ancient emperor) divided into three parts, the new SAT has been divided into Writing, Reading, and Math sections by the folks at the College Board (modern-day Caesars). Each section has several subsections, which clock in at more or less 25 minutes apiece, so that the test as a whole looks like this:

- Writing
  - Essay — two pages of terrifying white space
  - Editing — select the best way to rephrase parts of a sentence
  - Grammar — rules and regulations
- Reading
  - Sentence completions — vocabulary in context
  - Short articles — bite-sized chunks of semi-interesting material
  - Long articles — long, dull, and annoying reading passages
- Math
  - Multiple choice — math questions with selected answers
  - Grid ins — you're on your own in this one, no answers given

These categories are divided into sub-tests so that each section has a total of three sub-tests. This means that nine separate tests comprise the SAT. However, if this weren't enough, one extra test — called the dummy — is thrown into the mix.

The College Board uses the dummy to hype the SAT as a "statistically normalized" test, which allows them to throw in questions from old SATs, try out questions for new SATs and just generally make your life miserable by experimenting to their heart's content. All of this takes place on your dime. Since you have no idea which section of the SAT is the dummy (although it's usually an extra Math or Reading section), you have to treat all sections with the same due diligence.

The dummy brings the total number of sections you must finish on the new SAT to a mentally — and physically — exhausting total of ten. Roughly three hours and 45 minutes of SAT agony. And the worst part isn't finishing the test — it's getting started. Why? Here's the kicker — it's called white space. Read on.

White Space

When you open your test booklet for the SAT, you'll recall, the first thing staring you in the face is the essay — a mass of terrifying white space, two pages of lined paper waiting to be filled in with deathless prose. If you mess up here, panic overtakes you, and your score on the rest of the test suffers as well.

Two pages of terrifying white space

It's sort of like a basketball player missing his or her first couple of shots or a swimmer getting a slow start off the blocks. If you do poorly on the essay, you not only receive a low score on that portion of the test, but you also have a hard time recuperating and staying focused on the remainder of the SAT.

Conversely, if you nail the essay — and the vast majority of my students do — you move on into the rest of the test with confidence and purpose, knowing that you've got game and that the force is with you.

So, the essay is important not only on its own terms but also as a prelude to your performance on the rest of the test. Get off to a good start and enter the zone.

But what constitutes a good start and who says so?

Readers — Who are These People?

The College Board recruits high school and college teachers (typically, English teachers) to grade your essay, giving it a score from 1 to 6. Since two Readers are assigned to each essay, the top score is 12 — 6 from each reader.

At some point after the test has been scored, your essay, along with everyone else's, is scanned by a computer, turned into a PDF file and downloaded to an SAT database for eventual distribution to selected Readers.

Each reader receives a batch of essays and begins the scoring process. Now, do you suppose the Readers are going to grade your essay in the same way they grade class papers; that is, with meticulous attention to detail and a surplus of red ink? Absolutely not.

Readers get paid by the hour and the more essays they grade, the more chance they have of being invited back to participate in future essay-grading marathons. Therefore, the incentive for the reader is to move through each essay as swiftly as possible, spending no more than 2 minutes per essay.

That's right. You spill your guts out under intense please-god-get-me-into-college pressure and your reader takes a leisurely stroll down essay lane grading your prose in less than 10% of the time it took you to write it.

On the surface this may seem twisted and unfair, but you can make it work to your advantage. Knowing Readers prefer to work fast, you can structure your essay to help them do just that.

Two things are essential in this regard:

- Making a good first impression with your opening paragraph
- Using clear transitions from front to back throughout your essay so that the reader can follow, Oz-like, the yellow brick road

More on these things later. First, let's take a look at the criteria employed by Readers to judge your essay.

Rules of Engagement

There are several commonly-agreed upon criteria for judging good writing. Collectively these comprise a rubric or a set of rules employed as a scoring guide. These include:

- Structure — your essay must follow the classic five-paragraph format; that is, an introductory paragraph, three body paragraphs, and a conclusion
- Topic Sentence — your intro paragraph must have a clearly defined topic sentence or thesis
- Transitions — your essay must have smooth transitions (remember, guide the reader down the proverbial yellow brick road) both between paragraphs and within paragraphs
- Subordination — good prose style is characterized by heavy use of subordination. Subordination lends variety to your writing style by replacing short, choppy, subject-verb-object sentences with longer, more elegant sentences that incorporate dependent clauses. Take the following examples of two boring subject-verb-object sentences stuck together with a period.

Rosa Parks refused to give up her seat on the bus. She inspired the Civil Rights movement.

There are three different ways to rearrange and subordinate these choppy sentences to make them more interesting. For example:

- After refusing to give up her seat on the bus, Rosa Parks inspired the Civil Rights movement.

  Notice the long lead-in *After refusing to give up her seat on the bus,* which now precedes the subject of the sentence, Rosa Parks. This is a much better use of sentence variety.

- Rosa Parks, an inspiration to the Civil Rights movement, refused to give up her seat on the back of the bus.

  In this example, the inserted phrase *an inspiration to the Civil Rights movement* is now sandwiched, to much greater effect, between the main subject and verb of the sentence.

- Rosa Parks refused to give up her seat on the back of the bus, inspiring the Civil Rights movement.

  In this example, the tag-along to the main clause *inspiring the Civil Rights movement* is now placed at the end of the sentence, creating smoother sentence flow.

Technically, these last two examples utilize appositives to achieve subordination, but in this book I define subordination as any phrase or clause that is not necessary for the main sentence to stand on its own. Grammarians, take note

Regardless, in all cases subordination is the mark of an excellent writer. The more subordination, the more elegant the prose.

- Flash vocabulary — impress the reader with your use of interesting and sophisticated vocab sprinkled throughout your essay
- Concrete Examples — no matter how good your writing style, you need familiar examples from American history, literature and technology to support your thesis. Otherwise, the writing is just hot air. But don't worry, dozens of sample paragraphs (content examples) are provided in later chapters.

As I say, these six criteria for judging an essay comprise a commonly accepted academic standard. That's all well and good; however, it should be pointed out that the College Board, in its infinite wisdom, publicly denies adherence to this — or any — rubric.

Instead, the College Board advises that each essay will be judged *wholistically*. Come again? That's right, wholistically. In other words, subjectively. Wholistically is just a cover, a subterfuge, a sneaky back-door admission by the test makers that they won't be pinned down or held accountable for any rubric whatsoever.

So what's really going on here?

No matter what the College Board publicly proclaims, it doesn't mean that Readers won't be applying the qualitative rules mentioned above — they will, they have to, they're academics! — it just means that another, strictly quantitative measure will also be applied, perhaps subliminally. That is:

- LENGTH

In the topsy-turvy world of the SAT essay, quantity seems to count as much as quality. So, no matter how good your prose, if the essay isn't long enough, your grade will suffer. It's not fair, I know, but — hey — we're here to deal with it. This means that, no matter what, you have to keep your pencil moving to eat up two pages of white space.

Adam Robinson, Princeton Review founder and SAT guru for over 20 years, advises his students to edge well past the 400 word mark. I agree with him and urge all my students to meet the 400 word mark for a minimum score of 10 on their essays. For an 11 or 12 (12 being a perfect score) I counsel at least 450 words.

No less an expert than Les Perelman from MIT, one of the official Readers-in-training for the SAT essay, had some interesting words to say about length as a indicator of essay success. In an interview with Linda Wertheimer from NPR, available on the web, Perelman states:

> After I was given the (essay) samples at this conference, I went back to my hotel room and started going through it, and when I got to the ungraded samples, I realized I could score it before I read it because just a certain length was always a certain score. So being from MIT, where numbers are very important, I counted the words, put the number of words and the scores into an Excel spreadsheet and discovered that the correlation was the highest I've ever seen in test data

So there you have it. Not only are you required to write a qualitatively sound essay, applying the previously mentioned rules of engagement, but you're also expected to chew up every inch of white space available on two lined pages.

What if you write big, some of my students have inquired. Tough luck, is the unfortunate answer. To ensure you get at least a score of 10 (which, by the way, is very good) you have to write small AND fill up the white space.

Because the essays are graded subjectively — sorry, I mean *wholistically* — there are, of course, exceptions. But to be on the safe side, I have all my students write small, write fast, and write smart. Which is what this book is all about.

And remember, over 30% of my students have received an 11 or 12 on the essay. If that weren't enough, my students *average* a 10, which is well above the national norm and definitely within reach of each and every reader. Using the techniques and methodology described in this book, ANYONE can learn to write a top-scoring essay.

In the ensuing chapters, I'll elaborate on specifics. First, however, let's take a look at the literary lay of the land.

2—Snapshot

≡

As the title suggests, this chapter is short and sweet. It's a quick overview of what an SAT essay should look like. In later chapters, I'll explain in gory, wide-angle detail how to prefabricate the component parts you need to build a successful essay from scratch. Right now, I'm more interested in taking a vertical approach, presenting an essay from top to bottom so you can see a clear beginning, middle and end.

As part of that process, I've also highlighted the component parts — building blocks - that go into the construction of the essay. Pay close attention to these since they are common to all good SAT essays and help the SAT Readers appreciate the logical progression and narrative flow that hold your supporting arguments together.

Sample Essay

That said, here's a sample essay written for the abbreviated prompt *Every Advance Involves Some Loss or Sacrifice.* This essay, derived from work produced by my students, has an introduction, three body paragraphs (examples from history, literature and personal experience) and a conclusion.

> Most people in America, if not the world, would agree that every advance involves some sacrifice. In fact, a common sports adage proclaims: "No pain, no gain." In other words, progress is always accompanied by a certain amount of loss. This concept is illustrated throughout history, literature and personal experience.
>
> One compelling illustration that some bad always accompanies some good is demonstrated in the Civil Rights movement. In 1955 Rosa Parks refused to give up her seat on the bus to a white person. Although she was arrested and jailed, her brave efforts inspired the Montgomery Bus Boycott which lasted for over a year. Martin Luther King was inspired by her example and became known as one of the most admired figures of the Civil Rights movement. He organized hundreds of non-violent protests and gave an unforgettable speech entitled "I have a dream." Martin Luther King and Rosa Parks helped get the

Civil Rights Act of 1964 passed. Unfortunately, this social progress was accompanied by a tragic sacrifice: the assassination of Dr. King by a southern madman.

The theme that every advance involves some loss also occurs in Nathaniel Hawthorne's novel, The *Scarlet Letter*. The protagonist, Hester Prynne, is charged with adultery and is forced to wear a scarlet letter "A" embroidered on her dress. Although the Puritan community shuns her for her sins, Hester decides to reform her character by doing selfless charity work. As a result of her philanthropic character, the society changes its view of Hester and eventually thinks of the scarlet "A" on her dress as representing the word, "Able." Through her hard work and sacrifice, Hester is able to move forward with her life and become a valued member of the community.

A final illustration that progress always involves a loss occurred in my own personal experience building houses in Mexico with my church group. During the summer of my junior year in high school, I traveled with a small group to Guadalajara to help construct low-income housing for the poor. At first, I was appalled at the extent of the poverty around me and longed to return home to enjoy the rest of my summer lounging by the swimming pool. However, these thoughts soon departed when we finally got to work. Arranged in teams, we developed a sense of common purpose and community spirit while helping those less privileged than ourselves. Consequently, I learned the value of hard work and group sacrifice. As our church leader remarked, "You give up a little, in order that other people may gain a lot."

As seen in these historic, literary and personal experience examples, every advance is accompanied by inevitable suffering. However, with perseverance and planning, even the worst setbacks can be overcome. This notion is particularly relevant to our lives today for the world is undergoing change at an alarming rate. As Franklin D. Roosevelt once said, "You may be disappointed if you fail, but you are doomed if you don't try."

So, there it is — a classic five-paragraph essay with a good intro, serviceable conclusion, and three re-usable content examples.

I say re-usable since these three content examples — Civil Rights, *Scarlet Letter* and the Church Group personal experience— contain sufficient acts of historical importance, social drama, obstacles overcome and challenges met to support almost all prompts that come your way. The trick, of course, is to know how to define the prompt to fit your content examples. To make this crystal clear, I include an entire chapter later in the book called *Spin the Prompt* (Chapter 8) that shows you how to deal with all possible SAT essay topics.

Moreover, to ensure you have a variety of content examples at your disposal (over and above Civil Rights, *The Scarlet Letter* and an example from personal experience) I include another chapter called *Details, Details, Details* (Chapter 7). This chapter provides content examples from other historical periods and literary works as well as examples from technology and personal experience.

In short, stick with the program, guys; in due time, you'll be well prepared for every possible SAT contingency.

Building Blocks

Every SAT essay is really just a series of building blocks stacked one on top of the other. One of the tricks to writing an essay in twenty-five minutes or less is knowing how to assemble these blocks quickly into a cohesive whole.

In this section, I walk through the snapshot essay from start to finish, highlighting the function of each of the major building blocks and showing, with snippets from the essay, how that function is put into play.

In other words, **notice how**:

- The introduction of the essay sets the scene with a broad, general statement, which is followed by a well-know quote that supplies context to the prompt.

    Most people in America, if not the world, would agree that every advance involves some sacrifice. In fact, a common sports adage proclaims: "No pain, no gain."

- The second-to-the-last sentence of the introduction defines the topic. This is your thesis statement and is the central point around which your essay revolves.

    In other words, progress is always accompanied by a certain amount of loss.

- The last sentence of the introduction acts as a transition to prepare the reader for the body paragraphs that follow.

    This concept is illustrated throughout history and literature.

- Each body paragraph starts with a transition sentence that recaps the topic.

    One compelling illustration that some bad always accompanies some good is demonstrated in the Civil Rights movement.

    The theme that every advance involves some loss is also demonstrated in Nathaniel Hawthorne's novel, The *Scarlet Letter*.

    A final illustration that progress always involves a loss occurred in my own personal experience building houses in Mexico with my church group.

- Each body paragraph supplies low-level supporting detail for the topic sentence.

  In 1955 Rosa Parks refused to give up her seat on the bus to a white person . . .

  The protagonist, Hester Prynne, is charged with adultery and is forced to wear a scarlet letter "A" embroidered on her dress . . .

  At first, I was appalled at the extent of the poverty around me and longed to return home to enjoy the rest of my summer lounging by the swimming pool.

- The conclusion starts with a transition sentence that recaps the topic.

  As seen in these historic, literary and personal experience examples, every advance is accompanied by inevitable suffering.

- The conclusion closes the sale with a general statement and a quote from an apparent authority that has some broad relevance to the topic.

  This notion is particularly relevant to our lives today for the world is undergoing change at an alarming rate. As Franklin D.Roosevelt once said, "You may be disappointed if you fail, but you are doomed if you don't try."

Key Point about Prompts

The key point to recognize in all of this is that these building blocks apply, in some degree or other, to *every* SAT essay. How can that be possible, you ask, when the prompts change for every test? Well, the trick is to understand that although every prompt *appears* different, they are all fundamentally the same. To paraphrase the French, when it comes to SAT prompts, the more things change, the more they stay the same.

Because the SAT is a national test, the prompts are generic, involving issues that lend themselves to different — and invariably conflicting — points of view. The easiest way to address such issues is to emphasize the dramatic elements inherent in the subject matter. As a result, regardless of the wording, all SAT prompts can be boiled down to themes involving one word: **DRAMA**. We've seen this already in the three content examples from our sample essay (Civil Rights, *Scarlet Letter* and the Church Group personal experience), all of which contain various elements of conflict, tension, and achievement: in short, drama.

Well, it turns out that this is the case for virtually every prompt. No matter what the prompt *appears* to say, you can address it using prefabricated content examples that interweave three basic motifs:

- Overcoming obstacles
- Meeting challenges
- Achieving progress — either individual, social or both

In the following chapters, we'll expand on this theme and explain how you can **prefabricate** the component parts of an essay ahead of time and spin them to address whatever topic the College Board throws at you.

Along the way, expect to see LOTS of examples from various students illustrating how these points are put into play. One of the key features of this book — and of my overall teaching methodology — is to use dozens of real-world essays to get you up and running as a successful SAT essay writer in the shortest possible amount of time.

3—Prefab Structure

In the previous chapter, we took a look at a snapshot essay and some component parts — building blocks — that were essential to structuring an SAT essay quickly and cohesively.

These building blocks are like the scaffolding and prefabricated structures used by workmen to put up large big-box stores overnight. You know what I mean: one day there's a vacant lot; next thing you know a Best Buy, a Home Depot or a Walmart has sprung up out of nowhere. What's the trick? Prefabrication.

Contractors pour cement foundations, raise pre-assembled frame walls, add standard joists and rafters, tack on a roof, and start rolling in the merchandise. Not a lot of hand-crafting or originality goes into the final product, but the job gets done fast and fairly well.

So it is with the SAT essay. Instead of creating an essay entirely from scratch, we're going to prefabricate a lot of the structural support. Remember, the College Board, in its infinite wisdom, has decided you get twenty-five and only twenty-five minutes to construct an essay. In the real world, of course, this is nuts! Real writers constantly edit, revise, and re-organize their compositions. A more realistic writing exercise would be for the College Board to give you another 15 minutes and extra space at the end of the SAT to return to your original essay and revamp it. Alas, this is not an option.

Therefore, to ensure success within a limited time frame, you have to be prepared to reach into your own personal Bag of Tricks and pull out appropriate prefabricated materials. Two of the most important of these are the **introduction** and **conclusion**, the twin towers of essay writing. They hold your essay together and give it the symmetrical shape Readers like to see.

In this chapter, I'll show you how to go about constructing these. But first, a few words about dealing with the SAT prompt.

The Prompt

Every SAT essay begins with a three paragraph prompt. The prompt usually contains a quote box from an authority on a given topic and a subsequent assignment.

In the previous chapter the prompt was summarized for brevity. Here is the same prompt (*Every advance involves some loss or sacrifice.*) as it might be displayed in an actual SAT test.

Think carefully about the ideas and issues presented in the following excerpt and assignment below.

In the famous 19th century novel, *Thus Spake Zarathustra*, the German philosopher Frederick Nietzche wrote: "That which does not kill me, makes me stronger." This well-known adage is often interpreted to mean that setbacks are a prelude to progress.

Assignment: What is your view of the idea that every advance involves some loss or sacrifice. In an essay, support your position with reasoning and examples taken from your reading, class studies, or personal experience.

Notice two important things here.

- The quote box is often wordy, abstract and intimidating
- Regardless of how wordy, abstract and intimidating the quote box may be, the thesis — in this case *every advance involves some loss or sacrifice* — will always be explicitly spelled out for you after the word **assignment**. (Thank God for small favors.)

To handle this (or any) prompt, take a deep breath and remember that no matter what the prompt, the three narrative motifs from the last chapter can be used to address it. Next take a minute to prepare an introduction and plot an overall plan of attack. We'll have a lot more to say about the specifics of this attack (and how to deal with variations in the prompt) later but for now some important words about getting started.

Introduction

Every SAT essay starts with an introduction, which consists of three parts:

- a general statement that sets the scene
- a specific thesis or topic sentence

- a transition to the first body paragraph

In *Apocalypse Now*, Francis Ford Coppola's introspective, dream-like anti-war movie, the opening shot depicts the lush Vietnam landscape turned into a fiery inferno as helicopters drop napalm on the jungle. The camera pans and scans across this conflagration, superimposing an inverted image of Captain Willard in a Saigon hotel room over the action, contrasting the external devastation in the jungle with the internal turmoil of the protagonist. Jim Morrison plays in the background.

The opening to your essay won't be anywhere near as fancy as this, but the **pan and scan** idea is at the heart of a good intro: in a couple of sentences you want to make a general statement that will both establish a tone and set the scene for the rest of your thesis.

Your objective here is to give the reader a cinematic, birds-eye-view of the proverbial forest, before zooming in on the prefabricated trees.

Here are a couple of examples of the how you can get this job done.

Sample Intros

Four different intros are presented here:

- The first sets the scene for the thesis by recounting an anecdote, which is just a fancy name for a short tale or an amusing biographical incident. In this case the story of R. H. Macy, the famous department store magnate, is described.
- The second quotes a common expression and, again, relates an anecdote — this time involving Thomas Edison, the well-know inventor.
- The third employs an interesting spin on the topic while employing both quotes and anecdotes of famous disabled individuals to provide purpose and sweep.
- The final intro uses a sweeping quote to set the scene, enlarges the scope to modern society and ends by introducing the two individuals whose lives will be explored in the ensuing paragraphs.

Intro One:

In many instances people attempt to succeed, yet end up failing. R. H. Macy, for example, went bankrupt seven times before he finally achieved financial success with the department store that now bears his name. Progress can be defined in many ways but it is best thought of as the act of moving forward onto new things or ideas regardless of the obstacles that stand in our way. In fact, every advance involves some loss or sacrifice. This concept is illustrated throughout history, literature and personal experience.

The trick here is to make a sweeping opening statement. Then follow that up with a historical anecdote that addresses the thesis in a *general* way, while leading the reader directly to a specific topic sentence:

> In fact, every advance involves some loss or sacrifice.

Directly after your topic sentence, provide the reader with a roadmap so they can easily apprise the route you plan to take in presenting your essay. The roadmap can be as simple as listing the type of content examples you intend to present:

> This concept is illustrated throughout history, literature and personal experience.

Intro Two:

> A famous proverb proclaims that: "If at first you don't succeed, try, try again". This profound advice suggests that failure is inevitable before success. Thomas Edison, for example, experimented with over 100 types of metal filaments before finally settling on Tungsten for the electric light. His success, in other words, didn't come overnight. It resulted from persistence and hard work. Put another way, every advance involves some loss or sacrifice. This concept is illustrated throughout history, literature and personal experience.

The strategy here is similar to that of the first intro but quotes a proverb before moving on to relate an anecdote about Edison, whose persistence in the face of adversity finally pays off. Notice, again, how this paves the way for the specific topic sentence:

> Put another way, every advance involves some loss or sacrifice.

As in the first sample intro, directly after your topic sentence, provide the reader with a roadmap, detailing the areas from which you plan to draw your content examples.

Intro Three:

> Winston Churchill once said "Mankind's greatest achievements stem from personal loss or sacrifice." Individuals like Helen Keller and Stephen Hawking overcame tremendous disabilities before going on to achieve professional and social triumph. Keller, born blind, deaf and dumb, became a premiere educator and spokesperson for the disabled. Stephen Hawking battled Lou Gehrig's disease to become the world's foremost theoretical physicist. Today Hawking activates a special keypad and uses a computer generated voice to communicate his ideas. Both these individuals refused to let personal loss stand in the way of progress. This concept can be further illustrated in history, art and science.

This intro employs both quotes and anecdotes to set the stage for the essay. It also gives a different spin to the idea of loss or sacrifice, using personal disabilities as a springboard to support the prompt. Remember, it's the way you spin the prompt that matters; it's not the prompt itself, it's your *interpretation* of the prompt that matters.

Intro Four

> Franklin D. Roosevelt, both a polio victim and the 32nd president of the United States, once stated, "Overcoming adversity is the hallmark of individuals who have shaped the world." Everyone faces obstacles in their lives, sometimes meeting challenges on a daily basis. Modern society is able to progress through the success of a few hardworking and innovative individuals who have the rare ability to seize the day and rise above the fray. Without these original and persistent individuals, our world would be dull, corrupt, and unvarying. Individuals like Civil Rights leader Martin Luther King and baseball great Jackie Robinson are just a few who demonstrate that every advance involves some loss or sacrifice.

Look how nicely this quote from FDR — real or imagined? Stand by, we'll discuss this later — supports the prompt and facilitates comment on society at large. The emphasis is then shifted to two specific individuals who personify the topic and whose lives will be explored in more detail during the body of the essay.

Chess Moves

Later in this book, we'll take a look at dozens of real-world introductions written by real students to give you a variety of openings for any given SAT prompt. Think of these as chess moves, of which whole books have been written, some with titles like *Standard Chess Openings*, which pretty much says it all. My favorite chess opening as a child was the Roy Lopez. Allowed me to kick butt when I played against other eight-year-olds, even older kids far smarter than I.

In any case, as I mentioned in the first chapter, seeing things done right by other people is an excellent way of learning how to get the job done right yourself. Every chess master is familiar with dozens of opening moves. Switch chess master to essay master and you, too, can join the club.

Simulation

Along these same lines — and to reminisce further — I remember a one-sided conversation I had back in the day with my high school English teacher, Father O'Laughlin. I broached the subject of learning different styles of poetry by simulating famous poems like Robert Browning's *My Last Duchess* or Keats' *Ode to a Nightingale*. That was the word I used back then: *simulating*.

"You mean copying," said Father O.

"Well, I mean writing in a similar style and sort of imitating the author."

Father O straightened the sleeve of his spotless Sacred Heart cassock and shot me a long look across the crowded classroom. "You mean *copying*," he said, with the finality of a national debate coach, which in fact he was.

I saw no point in bringing up Art Diaz and recounting my summer of basketball *simulation* and how it had paid big dividends when I had finally incorporated Diaz' moves into my own. That conversation was over.

But I want to make a point of it here. Brilliant, innovative writers have no need of imitation, templates, frames, models, hooks, or prefabrications. The rest of us, mere mortals, need help simply getting started. That's the main purpose of this book.

So, in the beginning, feel free to simulate, imitate or sample whatever words, phrases, sentences or paragraphs you find here; anything that will help you construct a cohesive essay. As you get more familiar with the content on display in this book, enter the zone and make it your own.

Conclusion

The conclusion of your essay is a mirror image of your introduction. Therefore, it consists of three parts:

- a transition from the last body paragraph
- a recap of the thesis or topic sentence
- a general statement that finalizes the sale

Every SAT writer is inherently a salesman. Your product is your twenty-five minute essay. Your job is to sell it to the SAT Readers. To do this successfully, take a page out of Alec Baldwin's book in *Glengarry Glenn Ross*. Confronting a raggedy-ass sales team desperately in need of motivation, he writes the following mantra on the office white board: *ABC — Always Be Closing.*

This advice is vitally important for each content example of your essay, as we'll see in the next chapter. But, for now, keep in mind that the conclusion is your final chance to close the sale.

At the end of *The Great Gatsby*, for example, F. Scott Fitzgerald eulogizes his ironic hero, a dreamer haunted by the past, blindsided by the future, and hopelessly entranced by the green light at the end of Daisy's dock. In the last line of the book, Fitzgerald pulls the camera back, so to speak, for a final long shot, which both summarizes Gatsby's plight and extrapolates it to the reader:

> Gatsby believed in the green light, the orgastic future that year by year recedes before us. It eluded us then, but that's no matter — tomorrow we will run faster, stretch out our arms farther . . . And one fine morning —
>
> So we beat on, boats against the current, borne back ceaselessly into the past.

Not just Gatsby, Fitzgerald seems to be saying here, but all of us, every American, we're all in the same metaphoric boat — a boat engulfed by broken dreams.

Now, Fitzgerald had more than twenty-five minutes to compose his ending. You don't. Therefore, you have to be prepared. This means you'll need a final transition and a sweeping statement at the end of your essay that has broad relevance to your thesis.

The transition that begins your final paragraph is just a recapitulation of the roadmap you provided for the reader at the end of your introductory paragraph. For example:

> As the previous historical, technological and personal experience examples have shown, every advance involves some sacrifice.

Along the same lines, the first sentence of your final paragraph could simply repeat the actual content examples you provided. For example:

> As the previous examples from Civil Rights, Women's Rights and personal experience have demonstrated, every advance involves some sacrifice.

For maximum effect (and a top score) follow up your last transition with a sweeping statement that resonates with your topic. Quoting important people in your life or historical figures is always a good way to get this job done.

Sample Conclusions

Two different conclusions are presented here:

Conclusion One

> As we have seen in the lives of Martin Luther King, Susan B. Anthony and my own experience in Mexico, progress is not possible without sacrifice. For every two steps forward, individuals and society have to endure one step

backwards. Sacrifice governs our everyday activities and is necessary to move forward. As my grandfather, a champion boxer, was fond of saying: "Endure the pain, appreciate the gain."

Think back for a moment on what you've already learned about writing an introductory paragraph. You should be struck by the fact that your concluding paragraph, as presented above, is in fact a mirror image of your intro. This structural symmetry is the mark of an excellent SAT essay.

The folksy quote from the grandfather is also a nice touch. But do you really have a champion grandfather? And did he really come up with the quote you used to conclude your essay? Read on.

Conclusion Two

> As the previous historical, literary and personal experience examples have shown, every advance is accompanied by inevitable suffering. However, with perseverance and planning, even the worst setbacks can be overcome. This notion is particularly relevant to our lives today for the world is undergoing change at an alarming rate. As Franklin D. Roosevelt once said, "You may be disappointed if you fail, but you are doomed if you don't try."

This conclusion also mirrors your introduction but in a more abstract way, citing history, literature and personal experience as categories rather than specifying individual names within those categories. Either approach is fine. And like the previous example, the conclusion ends with a nice quote, this time a famous quote from FDR. Or is it?

Concluding Quote — Fact or Fiction?

Both sample conclusions end in quotes that are apparently real. A concluding quote from a famous authority — or a not-so-famous grandfather — is always a nice way to impress the reader and finish off your essay. But check this out: do accuracy and attribution really count on your essay?

The surprising answer is *no*. The Readers are instructed to grade your essay *wholistically* — remember that evasive word? — which means that they are instructed to ignore inaccuracies in an essay in order to concentrate on structure and overall presentation.

As a result, if you mess up on dates, names and places in your essay — at least within reasonable limits — no points are taken off. You can use this to your advantage.

Let's take a closer look at the FDR quote.

> As Franklin D. Roosevelt once said, "You may be disappointed if you fail, but you are doomed if you don't try."

Did FDR really say this? **In fact, no.** Does it matter that FDR never said this? Again, the answer is no. What matters is that *it sounds like* something FDR might have said.

In reality, this quote is from Beverly Sills, a famous soprano and former general manager of the New York City Opera.

My point here is extremely important: if the quote makes sense in the context of your essay and you can't remember who actually said it — should that stop you from using it? Absolutely not! All my students have used this principle to great advantage on their SAT essays.

Remember, the College Board has given you a chintzy twenty-five minutes to finish your essay with no recourse to outside materials. If this were a research paper, for example, you'd have time to read books and search the net to find — and cite — supporting arguments. If this were a newspaper article, you'd have a chance to check your notes and review your quotes. Here you have nothing: no time, no access to outside resources, no library stacks, no magazine index, no Internet. Zilch. Zip. Nada.

To put this in perspective, think back to Harrison Ford's cryptic remark when asked about his next move in *Raiders of the Lost Ark*: **"Look, pal. I'm making this up as I go along."** So are you.

You fight back with the only literary weapons at your disposal — fantasy and imagination. And this goes for quotes anywhere in the essay, not just the conclusion.

Moreover, you're in good academic company here. The maestro himself, Einstein, once famously remarked: "Imagination is more important than knowledge".

Strictly speaking, therefore, your essay may be considered a hybrid — partly fact, partly fiction. If Beverly Sills doesn't leap to mind, your go-to guy is FDR, a virtual repository of famous sayings.

Some of my top-scoring students have even taken this principle a step further and not only made up their own quotes to fit a specific prompt, but also attributed the quote to a non-existent person. Like a champion-boxer grandfather! My considered street-side response to this provocative act of literary fabrication is: Word.

Remember, the SAT Readers are trained **NOT** to count factual inaccuracies or content mistakes against you. By making up quotes you are perhaps stretching the limits of the essay, but you are nonetheless playing within the rules of the game.

Still, skeptical? Here's a link to an LA Times article by Karin Klein entitled, appropriately enough, *How I Gamed the SAT*

  http://articles.latimes.com/2005/apr/03/opinion/op-sat3

If, for whatever reason, you have qualms about gaming the system in this way, please refer to Chapter 6, *Quotes,* for a list of real-world quotes by real-world individuals, which you can use in a variety of contexts to support your thesis. Or simply attribute the quote to yourself; after all, you made it up!

4—Prefab Content

In fourth grade, I was not the smartest kid in the class. Pretty much an iconoclastic brat, I spent most of my time reading comic books: *Batman, Green Lantern,* and (my favorite) *Tommy Tomorrow.* Tommy was a precursor to William Shatner in *Star Trek,* broad shoulders, strong jaw, Bob's Big-Boy hair do. My hero. I read every Otto Binder episode and committed most to memory. My favorite was a tale of an eclectic group of aliens assembled by Tommy to help out a prospector on an isolated asteroid — kind of an intergalactic Dirty Dozen.

Curtis Bower, on the other hand, *was* the smartest kid in the class. Only ten, he had already made his way through "C" in the World Book Encyclopedia. Curtis's mom was obese and his dad rail thin. As children will, we took every occasion to tease him unmercifully with verses from Jack Sprat. Curtis, as you might imagine, was a nerd.

So it came as no surprise when Sister Germanus announced to the class that there had been two winners of the short-story contest and that one of them was Curtis Bower.

We had been asked to write up a two-page work of fiction based entirely on our imagination. Curtis had come up with a story about an adventure-loving uncle recently returned from Africa with a small box as a present for his nephew. The box contained a miniature, talking elephant, which became Curtis's prized pet. His story was imaginative and completely original.

I had re-written a Tommy Tomorrow episode about an eclectic group of aliens assembled to help out a prospector on an isolated asteroid. Sound familiar? I called it *The Strangest Space Crew in the Universe.* My story was imaginative but shamelessly derivative.

The day after we turned in our stories, Sr. Germanus walked briskly into the classroom with her black School-Sisters-of-Notre-Dame robes swirling around her and announced in a matter-of-fact voice: "As expected — and good morning to all of you — your stories from last night were atrocious. Weak. Worthless. Except for two. "

She went on to commend my work and Curtis' as exceptional pieces of kiddy prose. Later, after class, she took me aside and asked me where I had come up with the idea for my story.

"A comic book, s'tir". I could not tell a lie.

Sister eyed me resolutely, as though seeking divine guidance. After a long pause, she said: "Good start. A good effort. Not everyone's a Curtis Bower. Next time put a little more of yourself in it." Then she disappeared in a swirl of black.

Those words, I think, are relevant today. Not everyone's a Curtis Bower. Most people — people like us — need a little help getting started. A push. A prod. A jump start.

That's what this chapter's all about.

Raw Material

Katie Couric, the first female anchor on network nightly news, once gave some advice to college students on the benefits of a liberal arts education. To paraphrase Katie: It's as important to know **what** to write about as it is **how** to write it. Excellent advice.

In the previous chapter, we saw that a sweeping, **pan-and-scan** introduction and a well-defined thesis statement are the first order of business in any SAT essay. But what happens after that? Left to your own devices, how do you come up with the content examples you need to support your topic sentence? Where, in other words, do you obtain the raw material to populate your essay?

As with your introduction (and conclusion, for that matter), the answer is in large part *prefabrication*. There's no way around this. To build an intelligent, cohesive essay in twenty-five minutes or less you've got to start by prefabricating much of your response.

Toward this end, three of the best content examples to make yourself familiar with are:

- Civil Rights
- The *Scarlet Letter*
- Personal Experience

Civil Rights

No matter what prompt is presented to you on the SAT essay, you can use Civil Rights as an argument to support your position.

This works because SAT prompts are devised to challenge students to come up with supporting arguments for broad, open-ended propositions that can be interpreted in social terms. Moreover, since the SAT essay is an American test, students are expected to be familiar with key historical (as well as literary and technological) events that have influenced American society.

Civil Rights is a seminal event of 20th century America, an event that's impinged on the hearts and minds of everyone in this society.

Virtually all my students have used Civil Rights successfully as a supporting paragraph in their essays — regardless of the specific prompt given them.

So, where did they get their information? Some of them got it from school, when doing research papers. Others gathered information from the Internet and from each other in my classes by watching and doing.

To give an idea of how this works, let's return to the first body paragraph of our essay from Chapter 2 concerning Civil Rights and see where all that detail about Rosa Parks and Martin Luther King came from. Any ideas? The answer is simple: the Internet.

Here, for example, is a summary of facts relating to Civil Rights available to students on the Internet, courtesy of Professor Stanley K. Schultz at the University of Wisconsin-Madison (http://us.history.wisc.edu/hist102/lectures/lecture26.html).

- In 1955 Rosa Parks refused to sit in the back of the bus, prompting the Montgomery Bus Boycott. She was arrested and jailed
- In a march on Washington, D.C., Martin Luther King gave his inspirational speech "I have a dream."He was a proponent of non-violence and lead many marches and protests.
- In 1964, as a direct result of non-violent protests and demonstrations, Congress passed the Civil Rights Act, which outlawed discrimination.

From these facts, a thoughtful and provocative paragraph can be assembled.

Note: In this chapter, we'll stick to the same prompt we used in previous chapters: *Every advance involves some loss or sacrifice.*

One compelling illustration that some bad always accompanies some good is demonstrated in the Civil Rights movement. In 1955 Rosa Parks refused to give up her seat on the bus to a white person. Although she was arrested and jailed, her brave efforts inspired the Montgomery Bus Boycott which lasted for over a year. Martin Luther King was inspired by her example and became known as one of the most inspirational figures of the Civil Rights movement. He organized hundreds of non-violent protests and gave an unforgettable speech entitled "I have a dream." Martin Luther King and Rosa Parks helped

get the Civil Rights Act of 1964 passed. Unfortunately, this social progress
was accompanied by a tragic sacrifice: the assassination of Dr. King by a
southern madman.

The point to take home here is that you don't have to be an expert on the
complete history of Civil Rights in order to sound authoritative. A little
information, phrased well, goes a long way toward impressing the SAT Readers.

Note: For a view of Civil Rights from the perspective of the Civil War — and the
result amendments made to the Constitution — see Chapter 7, *Details,
Details, Details.*

Transitions

Another thing that impresses Readers is the use of transitions between
paragraphs. Recall that transitions are the super-glue that holds your essay
together. In the previous chapter, we saw a couple of important transitions for the
introduction and conclusion of your essay.

Providing transitions for the body paragraphs of your SAT essay is easy. Notice
how our Civil Rights paragraph begins:

> **One compelling illustration that** some bad always accompanies some good
> is demonstrated in the Civil Rights movement.

The text in bold represents the type of transition phrase that you can modify and
use in every SAT essay. Feel free to make up your own transitions since there are
multiple ways to smooth the flow between paragraphs. Once you have your
transitions down, the only thing that changes is the text you use to paraphrase
your topic sentence, which depends on the prompt provided.

Always Be Closing

One final point to consider. Recall Alec Baldwin's famous words from *Glengarry
Glenn Ross* referenced in the previous chapter: *ABC. Always be closing.* This applies
not just to your conclusion, but to each of your body paragraphs as well. It's
important, therefore, at the end of each body paragraph to return to the topic and
finish it off with a flourish. For example:

> Unfortunately, this social progress was accompanied by a tragic sacrifice: the
> assassination of Dr. King by a southern madman.

This not only wraps up the theme of the paragraph but also shows the reader that
you are on message. Readers dislike writers who deviate from their thesis and,
conversely, appreciate those that tow the line; which is to say, those that
demonstrate how their concrete examples support their topic sentence.

To garner reader appreciation (and receive a top score) *always be closing*.

Scarlet Letter

Along with Civil Rights, the other prime-time content example I require my students to have in their Bag of Tricks is a take on Hawthorne's *The Scarlet Letter*.

If you've read the book you already know the details. If you haven't, for purposes of illustration, let's suppose you've sifted through a variety of sources — the Internet, Cliff Notes, the movie (with Demi Moore and the *great* Gary Oldman), your friends, class discussions, whatever — and collected the following body of facts about the book:

- Hester Prynne, the unmarried protagonist, commits adultery with the Reverend Dimmesdale. A child (Pearl) is born out of wedlock
- The Reverend Dimmesdale keeps his affair with Hester secret from the Puritan community he ministers to. He is consumed with guilt and shame. His secret slowly devours him from the inside.
- As punishment for her sins, the community sentences Hester to wear a scarlet "A" (for adulteress) embroidered on her dress.
- Although shunned by the community, Hester openly accepts her fate and **transforms her personality**. She works diligently to make herself a productive member on the fringes of society doing needlework for the less fortunate and tending to her child. In the end, her selfless, charitable work endears her to the Puritan community.

Just as with the paragraph on Civil Rights, these simple facts can be assembled into a thoughtful and provocative paragraph.

> The theme that every advance involves some loss also occurs in Nathaniel Hawthorne's novel, The *Scarlet Letter*. The protagonist, Hester Prynne, is charged with adultery and is forced to wear a scarlet letter "A" embroidered on her dress. Although the Puritan community shuns her for her sins, Hester decides to reform her character by doing selfless charity work. As a result of her philanthropic character, the society changes its view of Hester and eventually thinks of the scarlet "A" on her dress as representing the word, "Able." Through her hard work and sacrifice, Hester is able to move forward with her life and become a valued member of the community.

Once again, you don't have to be an expert to sound authoritative. A little information, phrased well — and including transitions — goes a long way toward bagging you a top score.

Note: For another, more complex and sophisticated take on *The Scarlet Letter* — where the psychology of the main characters and the external/internal contrasts are highlighted — see Justin's essay in Chapter 9, *Go Fish*.

Transitions

Every body paragraph begins with a slightly different prefabricated transition. Here's what we used for our second body paragraph:

> **The theme that** every advance involves some loss **also occurs in** Nathaniel Hawthorne's novel, *The Scarlet Letter*.

The text in bold represents an all-purpose transition sentence that can be used in a variety of SAT essays. Again, the only thing that changes is the text you use to paraphrase your topic sentence.

Always Be Closing

By now you know your ABCs — so, once again, we conclude the paragraph with a flourish:

> Through her hard work and sacrifice, Hester is able to move forward with her life and become a valued member of the community.

Always be closing. You can almost hear the violins in the background. Crescendo. The curtain closes and the Readers stand up and applaud.

Personal Experience

The final type of content example to keep in your Bag of Tricks is one involving personal experience.

Although personal experience is not the best type of example to use to support your essay thesis, it nonetheless furnishes you with an acceptable fallback strategy. Just keep in mind that I advise my students to downplay personal experience and, if possible, use other types of content examples instead. Why is that?

In general, Readers seem to give higher marks to essays written with external (objective) supporting examples. However, in a pinch, if you can't come up with a third supporting example, you can always find a way to relate some personal experience — real or imagined — to fit the topic at hand. Just be advised you may have a harder time obtaining a perfect score. Nonetheless, you should still be in double digits.

That being said, I've included a sample personal experience paragraph below in order to give you an idea, if all else fails, of how to jump-start the writing process.

A final illustration that progress always involves a loss **occurred in my own personal experience** building houses in Mexico with my church group. During the summer of my junior year in high school, I traveled with a small group to Guadalajara to help construct low-income housing for the poor. At first, I was appalled at the extent of the poverty around me and longed to return home to enjoy the rest of my summer lounging by the swimming pool. However, these thoughts soon departed when we finally got to work. Arranged in teams, we developed a sense of common purpose and community spirit while helping those less privileged than ourselves. Consequently, I learned the value of hard work and group sacrifice. As our church leader remarked, "You give up a little, in order that other people may gain a lot."

Did the church leader really say that? Who knows. For that matter, did the summer excursion to Mexico really occur or was it just made up to reinforce the topic and provide a compelling content example? My answer is: who cares. The point here is that this personal experience logically (and vividly) supports the topic; whether it is fact or fiction makes no difference. Recall Einstein's famous injunction: "Imagination is more important than knowledge".

This being the case, you're advised to prepare (or *prefabricate*) a couple of personal experience examples for possible fall-back use in your essays. Prepare for the SAT essay the same way you prepare for SAT vocabulary. Commit as mush as possible to memory before the test. Be a boy scout. Be prepared.

Also note that if you do decide to insert a personal content example in your essay, be sure to tell the reader what you *learned* from the experience.

Consequently, I learned the value of hard work and sacrifice.

One of the key points to composing a personal experience paragraph is to show the Readers that you've grown, progressed or gained some perspective on events from the experience. That it's not just about you. That, as a result of the experience, you can see yourself as part of a larger picture. Family-of-man sort of thing.

Finally, notice that, for the first time in an SAT essay, you can use the pronoun "I". This is only allowed in a personal experience paragraph. At all other times, maintain objectivity by using "we" rather than "I".

Transitions

Let's review the final prefabricated transition used for the last body paragraph.

A final illustration that progress always involves a loss **occurred in my own personal experience** building houses in Mexico with my church group.

As you've probably noticed, this is roughly the same transition used for our other content examples. Only the supporting details have been changed. That's the beauty of prefabricating your transitions — you hit the ground running with each new paragraph, never having to stop and worry about how you're going to get started.

Always Be Closing

Also notice (one last time) how the paragraph comes full circle at the end, with the final quote reinforcing the main topic of the essay.

> In the end, I learned the value of hard work and sacrifice. As our church leader remarked: "You give up a little, in order that other people may gain a lot."

Content Examples

In addition to having both historical, literary and personal experience prefabricated content in your Bag of Tricks, you should consider having two other types of examples to draw from. These are:

- Pop culture
- Technology

Following is a short list of some common content examples, organized by topic, in categories we've already discussed.

History

- Civil Rights
- Women's Rights
- American Revolution
- Great Depression

Literature

- *Scarlet Letter*
- *Grapes of Wrath*
- *Great Gatsby*
- *To Kill a Mockingbird*

Personal Experience

- Building low-income houses with church groups
- Camping trips with the Scouts
- Drama club

We'll be looking at these and many others in much more detail in Chapter 7, *Details, Details, Details.*

And in Chapter 8, *Spin the Prompt*, I'll show you how to use your newly-constructed content examples to support **any** possible prompt that the College Board throws your way.

But for now, let's take a quick look at ways to incorporate these two additional categories — Pop Culture and Technology — into your repertoire.

Pop Culture

Some kids shy away from literature and resonate more comfortably with street-side entertainment such as movies, music, sports, art, TV shows, comic books, even children's books (Dr. Suess). No worries. If literature is not your thing, you can easily fall back on pop culture to provide appropriate content for your SAT essay.

Incorporating music, movies, and sports into the mix, for example, makes writing an SAT essay a piece of cake.

Music

Everybody has a favorite singer or rapper. So, put down your iPod, open up *Rolling Stone* or the *Source*, get a little background material and construct a music-oriented content example, the gist of which you can spin for any SAT prompt. Teen-age girls, for example, are big on Taylor Swift. Check it out.

> A final example of overcoming adversity to achieve success is illustrated by the story of country singing sensation, Taylor Swift. Taylor grew up in a deprived Pennsylvania household, depressed and lonely. After suffering through dozens of record-label rejections, Taylor was finally signed to Big Machine Records in 2004 and has since revolutionized the music industry. Before Swift, country music was filled with boring lyrics about guys in pickup trucks with their dogs. Taylor completely changed this concept by creating a new genre of music, a hybrid of that combined rock and country. Taylor's songs talk about tough breakups, beginning life at a new school, and constant adolescent turmoil. Teen girls have said that whenever they have a bad day, they can listen to one of many Taylor Swift songs and know that they are not alone. By converting her experiences of loss and sadness into songs such as *Teardrops on My Guitar*, Taylor Swift has changed the way that people listen to music.

Note: If Taylor Swift is not your idea of a street-smart music icon, then take a look at Conner's essay on Tupac Shakur in Chapter 9, *Go Fish.*

Movies

Don't have time to read *To Kill a Mockingbird* or *The Grapes of Wrath*? No problem. See the movie instead; the plot lines are similar enough to provide sufficient content. Even better, use a current blockbuster as your content example.

Blockbusters have all the basic ingredients of a good SAT essay: tension, drama, obstacles overcome, challenges met, and progress achieved. A lot of my students used Avatar to good advantage when the film first came out. Others used various and sundry super-hero films. Here's an interesting psychological take on Chris Nolan's second Batman movie.

> One convincing example that progress is only capable through sacrifice is shown in the movie, *The Dark Knight*. Throughout the film, the heroic vigilante Batman faces his arch-nemesis, the Joker, an anarchist whose sole purpose is to "set fire to the establishment." The idea of a masked vigilante seems to threaten the citizens of Gotham City because Batman acts as though he is above the law. Instead, the people of Gotham turn to District Attorney Harvey Dent, a man so untainted from corrupt business that he is coined the "White Knight." Towards the end of the movie, the Joker's ability to manipulate the emotions of others eventually transforms Dent into something different than the public perceives him, a two-faced madman. Upon Dent's death, in order to preserve the image of Dent as someone who can be the driving cause for change, Batman takes the blame for his death by assuming the role as the "Dark Knight." Although Batman loses his heroic image by becoming a convict, this sacrifice preserves and improves the lives of the citizens of Gotham City.

Sports

T. S. Elliot once said: "Most men lead lives of quiet desperation." The sports fan is an obvious — and loud — exception to this tenet. Desperate, maybe. Quiet, never. All it takes to write a top SAT essay is to channel this energy off the field into a nice content example with sufficient conflict, drama and social progress. The following example gets bonus points for combining racial justice AND sports in one finely crafted package.

> Another idea that supports the theme that no progress is capable without sacrifices occurs within the sports world. A common sports adage that every athlete will hear at least once in his or her lifetime is, "no pain, no gain." But for some famous athletes, this means more than merely putting blood, sweat and tears into something they love. One fine example of a person who overcame more odds than any other Major Leaguer is Jackie Robinson. A black male in a time of segregation and racial hatred, Jackie put his life on the line in order to play American baseball in the Major Leagues. Hounded by constant death threats, Jackie Robinson became a man determined to act as a

symbol of change and progress for all people of color. His ability to face the immeasurable pressures, threats, and criticisms of racism shows that every mortal must sacrifice something in order for others in society to progress.

Technology

OK, no SAT writing guide would be complete without some nod to nerds. You know, the guys who prefer TI-89s to iPhones, program Java rather than drink it, and take BC calculus for fun senior year. Guys for whom UC Berkeley is a safety school! Hey, no problem, there's room for everyone here. And SAT Readers, in particular, are always impressed by students with a scientific turn of mind, often awarding them top scores.

Chernobyl

A lot of students learn about the explosion at the Russian nuclear power plant at Chernobyl in chemistry class, where a film is often shown that details the destruction. If you've seen it, you may remember some of the facts.

If not, as a nerd, you might be interested in reading the blog of a motorcycle-driving Russian girl (Elena), who speed-trips through the deserted ghost-streets of Chernobyl for fun and relaxation! No joke. Of course, she keeps a geiger counter handy at all times to measure radiation levels so she doesn't get sucked into a hot zone. This girl's a trip, man; plus, she keeps a photo-journal of her travels!

So let's say you've checked Elena out at *http://www.kiddofspeed.com/chernobyl-revisited/chapter1.html* and read through her blog to uncover the still-riveting facts regarding Chernobyl. Now you're ready to put those facts into play as a detailed content example for your essay. Here's how it might look.

Note: For a shorter, but much less provocative explanation of what happened at Chernobyl, you can access Wikipedia at:
http://en.wikipedia.org/wiki/Chernobyl_accident

> Another illustration that progress is accompanied by sacrifice can be seen in the meltdown at Chernobyl, Russia. Before this tragic accident, Chernobyl was one of the leading nuclear power plants in the world. However, a series of operator actions, including the disabling of automatic shutdown mechanisms, led to the release of deadly radiation into the atmosphere. This left hundreds dead and caused severe fallout all over the city and as far away as Sweden. Even though Russia made lengthy progress in nuclear power, its citizens were met with sacrifices: thirty people killed and thousands sick with radiation poisoning.

Scientific Revolution

Anyone who's taken both AP Euro and Physics knows how to throw around words like *heliocentric* and *quintessential,* thereby impressing teachers, adults and, most importantly, SAT Readers. Here's what I mean:

> Another example in which innovative thinkers endure suffering to create progress is seen in the Scientific Revolution. The Scientific Revolution was brought about by creative thinkers and their breakthroughs in astronomy and physics. Such contributions included Copernicus' heliocentric model of the universe, Galileo's creation of the experimental method, and Sir Isaac Newton's Law of Universal Gravitation. All these men suffered persecution because their findings refuted the Aristotelian view of the universe and thus defied the Church itself. Paving the way for the Age of Enlightenment and modern science, the creative minds of the Scientific Revolution were quintessential attributes to human progress and modern world views.

Summary

To summarize, here is a short list of content examples from pop culture and sports that can be woven into SAT essays:

Pop Culture
- Taylor Swift
- The Dark Knight
- Jackie Robinson

Technology
- Chernobyl
- Scientific Revolution

These are just a few examples of how my students have mined pop culture and technology for content examples to use in their SAT essays. These and many more examples are provided later in Chapter 7, *Details, Details, Details* and in Chapter 9, *Go Fish*.

Transitions within Paragraphs

One final word on transitions to conclude this chapter. So far we've seen how to prefabricate transitions to structure the space between content examples. Good transitions, we've seen, facilitate narrative flow.

However, along with devising transition phrases *between* paragraphs, you also have to distribute them *within* paragraphs. Transitions within paragraphs demonstrate an agile and flexible mind able to sustain logical arguments and handle the necessary twists and turns in an essay.

Readers, when grading essays, prefer a guided tour through your essay; they hate unnecessary digressions and unwarranted zig-zags. They want to get through your prose as quickly as possible.

Transition words within paragraphs are like signposts on a highway, clearly delineating for the reader the logical twists and turns in the development of an essay. Moreover, transitions are the mark of a mind that knows how to handle both sides of an argument, an attribute Readers are apt to reward with a high score.

Following is a list of common transitions, divided into those that propel the narrative forward (pro) and those that signify a counterpoint (con) or reverse direction to the argument.

Pro	Con
consequently	however
therefore	on the other hand
along the same lines	in contrast to
in fact	ironically
thus	although
in addition	yet
moreover	despite
so	unfortunately
furthermore	but

To emphasize the use of both types of transitions, I repeat a snippet from the personal experience paragraph we saw earlier. Transition words within the paragraph are in bold.

> At first, I was appalled at the extent of the poverty around me and longed to return home to enjoy the rest of my summer lounging by the swimming pool. **However**, these thoughts soon departed when we finally got to work. Arranged in teams, we developed a sense of common purpose and community spirit while helping those less privileged than ourselves. **Consequently**, I learned the value of hard work and group sacrifice. As our church leader remarked, "You give up a little, in order that other people may gain a lot."

Once you've mastered the art of using prefabricated transitions both between and within paragraphs, your essay score will benefit tremendously.

Epilogue

As you get more familiar with the prefabricated material I've put on display in this chapter (and continue to display in subsequent chapters), start to think about modifying the examples given to create your own unique content examples. Outside the artificial confines of the SAT essay, originality is the mark of an accomplished writer in the real world.

In fact, in Chapter 9, *Go Fish*, I include some essays written by my students that successfully break or modify the prefabricated template mold presented here — at least as far as possible within the twenty-five minute time constraint of the essay.

Just remember, I started out mining comic books for my fourth grade stories but eventually progressed to become a full-fledged writer with my own voice. Not necessarily a Curtis Bower but — to paraphrase Sister Germanus — one who eventually learned to put a little bit more of myself into the mix.

5—Real SAT Essays

OK, relax, we're done with the fundamentals. We've analyzed and categorized all the separate pieces that go into a successful SAT essay. To recap briefly, these include:

- A sweeping introduction (pan and scan) employing quotes (real or imagined) and/or anecdotes relevant to the prompt
- A clearly defined topic sentence
- Various transitions between paragraphs
- Various transitions within paragraphs (however, consequently, furthermore, etc.)
- Prefabricated content examples drawn from history, literature, personal experience, pop culture or technology
- A broad, general conclusion which is, roughly speaking, a mirror image of your introduction.

Now let's look at how some real-world students applied these principles and techniques in high-scoring actual SAT essays.

To get things started, here's a prompt from the October, 2005 SAT. As usual, the prompt is divided into three parts: an introduction, a quote box, and an assignment section.

Recall that the quotes may or may not be helpful — sometimes they're too wordy or abstract and just get in your way. In any case, no worries: the prompt is always summarized for you after the word *Assignment*.

October, 2005 Prompt

Think carefully about the ideas and issues presented in the following excerpt and assignment below.

I. Celebrities have the power to attract communities of like-minded followers; they provide an identity that people can connect to and call their own. Celebrities are trusted; they stand for certain ideas and values to which followers can express allegiance.

Adapted from William Greider, *Who Will Tell the People?*

2. Admiration for celebrities is often accompanied by contempt for average people. As we focus on the famous, other people become less important to us. The world becomes populated with a few somebodies and an excess of near-nobodies.

Adapted from Norman Solomon and Jeff Cohen, *Wizards of Media Oz*

Assignment: Is society's admiration for famous people beneficial or harmful? Plan and write an essay in which you develop your point of view on this issue. Support your position with reasoning and examples taken from your reading, studies, experience, or observations.

Pared-down to its bare essentials, the prompt inquires — *Is society's admiration for famous people beneficial or harmful?*

At first glance, this prompt may not seem to have much in common with the prompt we've been dealing with in previous chapters (*Every advance involves some loss or sacrifice*). But the text itself is not what's important — what's important is how you **spin the prompt** to make it fit your purposes.

Rather than dealing with the prompt in its entirety, first decide which position (beneficial or harmful) you want to support. Then determine how to *define* the prompt so that you can reach into your Bag of Tricks and pull out appropriate supporting arguments. What, for example, characterizes famous people?

Well, if you think about it, famous people could easily be defined as individuals who've performed some socially beneficial role in history or literature. Reaching into your Bag of Tricks, Martin Luther King would make a good candidate for a role model. So would Women's Rights advocates like Susan B. Anthony and

Elizabeth Cady Stanton. Finally, Hester Prynne of literary fame is someone with admirable qualities, despite (or perhaps because of) the scarlet letter embroidered on her dress. Once the prompt is defined in this fashion, you're ready to rock and roll.

Which is precisely the strategy employed by Alex S., one of my star students, who received a top score for her October, 2005 SAT essay. See what you think.

Alex's Essay (score = 12)

Susan Plyte once said "Everyone needs someone to look up to." In today's society it is more important than ever for people to have role models in which they can admire and examine beneficial qualities that may help them in their everyday life. The universal notion that famous people are beneficial is exemplified throughout history and literature.

One example of how well-known people can benefit today's society is seen through the Civil Rights movement. In 1962 four college freshmen entered a restaurant in which they would receive no service at. The news of their non-violent sittings spread across the nation and within two months thousands of students were participating in these sit-ins. Their efforts inspired the creation of the student non-violent coordinating committee. In 1961 Rosa Parks refused to sit in the back of the bus where blacks were forced to sit. Although she was arrested and jailed, her brave efforts inspired the Montgomery Bus Boycott which lasted for over a year. Martin Luther King is known as one of the most inspirational figures of the Civil Rights movement. He organized hundreds of non-violent protests and gave an unforgettable speech entitled "I have a dream." Martin Luther King, Rosa Parks, and the Greensboro lunch boy's brave efforts helped get the Civil Rights Act of 1964 passed. Their actions have inspired thousands of people to stand up for what they believe in and are excellent role models for people today.

Another example of how celebrities can be beneficial in today's society is seen through the women's suffrage movement. Alice Paul, Susan B. Anthony, and Elizabeth Cady Stanton motivated thousands of women to stand up for equality. They organized parades, protests, and wrote hundreds of letters in order to gain awareness to their cause. They encouraged and convinced people that sexism was not right and were main contributors in getting the 17th amendment passed- granting women the right to vote. These three women are still excellent role models for people to look to and have inspired men and women to speak out against the things that they do not agree with.

Literature also has great examples of famous people and how they can benefit society. In Nathaniel Hawthorne's novel *The Scarlet Letter* Hester Prynne, the protagonist in the book commits adultery and must forever wear a scarlet letter "A" sewn upon her bosom. However, her giving personality and helpfulness makes people begin to refer to the "A" as meaning "able." Hester Prynne is an excellent role model for today's society in showing that everyone makes mistakes and that it is what you learn and do from them that is really important.

The Civil Rights movement, women's suffrage movement, and *The Scarlet Letter* have all produced famous people who are great role models for today. It is important for people to have these men and women to look up to and be encouraged by.

Notice how Alex starts off with a quote from Susan Plyte that supports her definition of famous people as role models. I assume you're all familiar with the famous sociologist Susan Plyte? No, never heard of her? Well, neither had I. Alex not only made up the quote to fit the prompt — more precisely, her *definition* of the prompt — but she also made up the person to whom the quote was attributed. Apparently, she took to heart the notion that imagination is more important than knowledge.

Once her topic sentence was defined, she grabbed some prefabricated transition glue (*this universal notion, etc.*) to segue into her content examples. Using a few simple facts woven together nicely in the second paragraph, Alex set herself up to sound like an expert on Civil Rights. Is she an expert? Not really, but that doesn't matter for the SAT essay. She doesn't have to be. The point is to *appear* to be an expert and impress the reader.

Also, Alex gets her dates a little mixed up, citing 1961 rather than 1955 as the date Rosa Parks refused to take a normal bus ride. Not a problem; the Readers are instructed to ignore factual inaccuracies in essays. It's an essay, not a term paper.

You could also argue that her dates were somewhat out of chronological sequence — she should have mentioned Rosa Parks before she brought in the four college freshmen (the Greensboro boys). To all which I say: *of course*, she should have. And could have. That is, if she'd been given enough time to revise her essay.

However, since this is not a *real* writing exercise — where you are given a chance to revise and edit your work — and since LENGTH matters and TIME is of the essence, the strategy I teach is to cram in as much detail into each paragraph as quickly (and elegantly) as possible in order to beat the clock and — again — to impress the reader!

Alex went on to use women's right (Susan B. Anthony, Alice Paul, Elizabeth Cady Stanton) as her second content example and Hester Prynne from *The Scarlet Letter* — yeah, famous literary heroines are role models, too — as her third.

Always Be Closing

One thing Alex does really well in her essay is close out each of her body paragraphs with a flourish. The last sentence of each body paragraph is displayed below. Notice how she returns each time to the main theme — role models — to hammer the point home. This gives her paragraphs, and indeed her entire essay, a sense of narrative cohesion; she's on message and knows how to close the sale.

> Their actions have inspired thousands of people to stand up for what they believe in and are **excellent role models** for people today.

> These three women are still **excellent role models** for people to look to and have inspired men and women to speak out against the things that they do not agree with.

> Hester Prynne is an **excellent role model** for today's society in showing that everyone makes mistakes and that it is what you learn and do from them that is really important.

Topic Sentence Recap

As an aside, you may be wondering why we recap the topic sentence (or thesis) as often as we do in an SAT essay. Two reasons:

- Keep your pencil moving — remember, length is important and recapping the topic adds significantly to your word count.
- Let the reader know you're on message — it's important to stick to the prompt as you define it in your essay. Recapping the topic, especially at the end of each body paragraph, demonstrates to the reader that you are adhering to the prompt and following a clear, logical and consistent path. Remember, Readers want to get through your essay in the least amount of time and therefore hate to be led off topic into time-consuming cul-de-sacs.

≡

April, 2006 Prompt

Think carefully about the ideas and issues presented in the following excerpt and assignment below.

> A teenager challenges everything and, by forming habits of intellectual and emotional independence, makes himself or herself into an adult. In a similar way, all people can learn the behaviors that they need to become the people they want to be. We can all change ourselves—our behaviors, our goals, our relationships—because our potential for change is unlimited.
>
> Adapted from Richard Stiller, *Habits*

Assignment: Is our ability to change ourselves unlimited, or are there limits on our ability to make important changes in our lives? Plan and write an essay in which you develop your point of view on this issue. Support your position with reasoning and examples taken from your reading, studies, experience, or observations.

Before I show you how this prompt was handled by one of my students, I want to set the scene by posing a hypothetical question — Ever been at a party and had absolutely nothing to offer to the conversation?

Join the club. So what do you do? Probably make some lame attempt at sounding intelligent by talking music, sports, fashion, movies — whatever comes into your head.

Well, that may get you through the next party, but it's not going to hack it for the next SAT. The Boy Scout motto is "Be prepared". As we've seen, nowhere is this more important than for the SAT essay.

When I was teaching English Grammar and Composition to foreign students at St. Mary's College (SMC) in Moraga, California, I developed an interest in international politics and world affairs. I needed to have something to talk about when hanging out with students from around the world. So I took out a subscription to *Foreign Affairs* magazine and read it pretty closely.

I remember one article in particular about Latin American Debt. Not the sexiest topic imaginable but stay with me here for the story.

The article went into great detail about how Brazil, which had thumbed its nose at the International Monetary Fund (IMF) over outstanding debt and was about to declare bankruptcy — a novel idea for an entire country back then — had finally relented and was in the process of renegotiation with the World Bank. Admittedly dry, fairly complicated financial stuff.

Well, later that week I was at a faculty party and people were speaking in authoritative voices about the looming third-world economic crisis. Not much of a talker myself, I was nonetheless well-armed for the topic due to my current reading.

But before I had a chance to impress the crowd with my new-found knowledge, one of the teachers at SMC, a friend and a *great* talker, took the bull by the horns and gave a complete exposition on the subject, going into great detail on the economic circumstances of Brazil. Believe me, the man couldn't have been more impressive if he'd been privy to the IMF proceedings himself. He sounded like a complete expert. For all intents and purposes, he *was* a complete expert.

The thing is, his talk seemed to have come directly from the article I had just been reading in *Foreign Affairs*. It wasn't a word-for-word recital — the teacher injected his own truth into the mix — but the structure, logic and details of his presentation were exactly those of the article's author.

So I ask you: was it unfair of the teacher to crib so extensively from someone else's work and present it as his own? Not at all is my answer. He'd absorbed the subject matter completely and, in the retelling, had made it his own. Sure, you can argue that some acknowledgement of the source material would have been nice to furnish to his listeners. Nice, but that's not the way the world works, at least not usually. People just don't walk around citing sources in their conversations.

Personally, I tend to be a little more scrupulous when it comes to attribution. In fact, I've used attribution quite extensively in this book, quoting both sources and authors. But my point is that people often bank off of other people's ideas and make them into something new, interesting and potentially more provocative.

And that's exactly what Tara T., another of my star pupils, has done in her April, 2006 SAT essay. She took my class, mastered the idea of prefabrication and took advantage of precedents — just like good lawyers do — to fashion her response to that month's SAT prompt.

You can argue that her essay — which follows — borrows extensively from Alex's essay. True, but that shouldn't be construed as a criticism. In fact, that's exactly what I taught her to do.

═

Tara absorbed the lessons of those that went before her (Alex S. and others), incorporated the salient details into her own experience, spun the April prompt to her own advantage, perfected the art of prefabrication and turned out an excellent SAT essay.

As Sir Isaac Newton famously proclaimed: "If I have seen further it is by standing on the shoulders of giants."

Well, Tara was no slouch when it came to shoulder standing. Moreover, she made it look easy, the mark of a well-schooled and talented writer. Take a look and judge for yourself.

Tara's Essay (score = 12)

As Richard Stiller once said, "We can all change ourselves — our behaviors, our goals, our relationships — because our potential for change is unlimited." There are no limits to the ability to make important changes. As a famous adage says, "Anything is possible, if you just set your mind to it." This universal notion is exemplified through history and literature.

One compelling illustration that change is unlimited is seen in the brave souls of the Civil Rights movement. In 1961, Rosa Parks refused to sit in the back of the bus, where blacks were forced to sit. Although she was arrested and jailed, her efforts led to the development of the Montgomery bus boycott, which lasted over a year. Then, in 1962, four college freshmen went into a restaurant and held a non-violent sit-in. News spread throughout the nation, and in two months, hundreds of college students participated in non-violent sit-ins. The Greensboro lunch boys efforts led to the development of the student non-violent coordinating committee. Martin Luther King Jr., one of the most famous leaders of the Civil Rights movement, organized many non-violent protests. His unforgettable and inspiring speech entitled, "I have a dream", encouraged thousands to stand up for what they believe in. Rosa Parks, Martin Luther King and the Greensboro lunch boys wanted change in their lives and the lives around them. They were unlimited in their efforts and fought hard for the change they desired.

Alice Paul, Susan B. Anthony and Elizabeth Cady Stanton were three women who worked hard for change they wished to see in the women's suffrage movement. They led parades, protests and even wrote letters on the incorrectness of sexism. Ultimately, they achieved their goal of passing the 17th amendment, granting women the right to vote. These three brave and courageous women fought consistently for the change they wanted in their lives, until it was achieved.

A final illustration that change is unlimited occurred in Nathaniel Hawthorne's *The Scarlet Letter*. The protagonist, Hester Prynne, commits adultery and is forced to wear an embroidered letter "A" on her bosom. Hester is shunned from the town and perceived as an outcast. However, Hester's giving and helpful personality is revealed and soon her "A" stands for "able" instead of "adulteress". Hester wanted the Puritan town to see a change and a different side to Hester's life, and through her hard work, she achieved that goal.

As seen in the Civil Rights movement, the women's suffrage movement and *The Scarlet Letter*, change is unlimited to those who wished to obtain it. As Sir Edward Bulwer once said, "Improvement can only be achieved by great change."

In her introduction, Tara makes an unusual but inspired move. Rather than trying to come up with her own quote to get the essay ball rolling, she instead quotes the quoter, Richard Stiller. This is a brilliant ploy, since it gets her pencil moving right away and allows her to leverage information provided by the College Board in the prompt to structure her essay. Smart girl, she's taking the game right back at them!

And for good measure, she adds an adage of her own: "Anything is possible, if you just set your mind to it." This allows her to move seamlessly into her content examples, using Civil Rights, Women's Rights and *The Scarlet Letter* to support her thesis that change is unlimited. These, of course, are the same three content examples used by Alex S. but now recast in a totally different context.

In fact, you should be struck by the way Tara used the same content examples as Alex but spun them to support a different prompt. Now, just to be clear, I'm not recommending that everyone recycle Civil Rights, Women's Rights and *The Scarlet Letter* for every essay; I just want to point out that having a variety of different content examples (five or six) in your Bag of Tricks will prepare you for any SAT essay eventuality.

Back in the day (circa 2005 and 2006, when Alex and Tara were writing their essays) this diversity of content examples was not necessarily *de rigueur* in obtaining a top score. However, by 2008, so many of my students were using and reusing these same content examples that one overzealous reader for the College Board actually accused a group of kids at one test center of "unusual similarities" in their writing, a euphemism some less-charitable members of the community hastily construed as "cheating".

The charge was bogus, of course; kids were just spinning common academic content examples — Civil Rights, Women's Rights, *The Scarlet Letter* — into their SAT essays as supporting arguments. But the College Board, a monolithic institution deemed otherwise. It unilaterally rescinded scores and demanded a re-test, subjecting my students and their parents to untold astonishment and grief. Trust me, Kafka has nothing on the College Board.

Long story short, I now stress diversity of content examples in my program so that kids don't inadvertently mirror each other's content examples in their compositions. And what happened, you might wonder, to those students forced to re-take the exam? Well, after some quick "diversity training" for the group on my part, they ended up aceing the retest, increasing their scores over 100 points and sticking it to the College Board in the process!

Always Be Closing

Finally, notice that Tara, like Alex, made a point to recap her thesis and close out each of her body paragraphs with a flourish.

> They were **unlimited in their efforts and fought hard for the change** they desired.

> These three brave and courageous women **fought consistently for the change** they wanted in their lives, until it was achieved.

> Hester wanted the Puritan town to **see a change** and a different side to Hester's life, and through her hard work, she **achieved that goal**.

> As Sir Edward Bulwer once said, **"Improvement can only be achieved by great change."**

I particularly like Tara's final quote to finish off the essay and close the sale. She may have been channeling Sir Edward Bulwer-Lytton, the prolific Victorian novelist, or she may have simply made the quote up. In either case, it's the perfect way to conclude her essay. A fadeout with finality.

May, 2007 Prompt

Think carefully about the ideas and issues presented in the following excerpt and assignment below.

There is an old saying: "A person with one watch knows what time it is; a person with two watches isn't so sure." In other words, a person who looks at an object or event from two different angles sees something different from each position. Moreover, two or more people looking at the same thing may each perceive something different. In other words, truth, beauty, may lie in the eye of the beholder.

Adapted from Gregory D. Forster, *Ethics: Time to Revisit the Basics*

Assignment: Does the truth change depending on how people look at things? Plan and write an essay in which you develop your point of view on this issue. Support your position with reasoning and examples taken from your reading, studies, experience, or observations.

At first glance, this prompt may seem different from those presented thus far, but in fact it just invites the writer to set up contrasts between conflicting social, historical and literary views. The usual suspects — Civil Rights, Women's Rights and *The Scarlet Letter* — are all content example candidates again.

But my next student, star pupil Alaizah K., took a slightly different tack and followed the advice of my fourth-grade teacher, Sister Germanus, to put a little bit more of herself in the mix.

Alaizah, who had just finished a term paper on the Spanish American War for History class, was consequently well-prepared to handle this SAT topic from a historical perspective and ended up producing an innovative paragraph dealing with William Randolph Hearst's manipulation of war for profit. Remember, no matter what the prompt, as long as your content examples include some mix of obstacles overcome, challenges met and progress achieved (in this case you can substitute profit for progress!) you're set to obtain a top score.

Alaizah used Civil Rights as a fall-back option in her second body paragraph, shifting the focus to the aftermath of the Civil War rather than the 1960s. And she finished up with *The Great Gatsby*, which she'd read in English class, highlighting the ambiguities inherent in the American Dream. All good stuff. Check it out.

Alaizah's Essay (score = 12)

Walter Worthington once proclaimed, "the truth, no matter the circumstances, will always remain ambiguous." In other words, the truth, intention or purpose of something will always be an opinion, and therefore remain uncertain. Throughout history, human beings have fought wars and pursued admirable dreams, but the perceptions of the intentions of these efforts have differed immensely. This universal notion that the truth changes depending on how one looks at something is exemplified throughout literature and history.

One compelling illustration that someone's intention could differ depending on the perspective is the Spanish American War. In the 1890's, Cuba, oppressed by the Spanish, valiantly fought for their independence. The United States sympathized with the striving nation, as they reminded us of our colonial days under Great Britain's rule. We decided to stand alongside Cuba and help them gain freedom. One perspective of this war could have been that America was performing a heroic, admirable deed. However, as New York Journalists, Pulitzer and Hearst, wrote in their newspapers, "you furnish the pictures, we'll furnish the war", the Cubans found our involvement quite selfish and imperialistic. We began to take advantage oft he Cubans after defeating Spain. We established the Teller Amendment (ensuring America's freedom and control in Cuba) and benefited from their economic resources and geographic location. We see from this example that depending on he person, Cuban or American, the SPAM War's truth and real intention could be greatly disputed.

Another example which demonstrates the theme the truth depends on the perspective is life after the Civil War. After we fought for African American rights, we established the 13th, 14th, and 15th amendments. These guaranteed their freedom, voting rights, and laws against discrimination. However, there was little truth to this kind of justice. Even though African Americans were no longer slaves, they were still subject to discrimination, Jim Crow laws, lynchings, and the Grandfather clause, which prohibited their right to vote. Depending on a Northerner's or an African American (viewpoint), Reconstruction and Civil Rights may or may not have truly served justice to the African Americans in the early 1800s.

A final example that the truth differs depending on the person is Hawthorne's novel *The Great Gatsby*. One may argue that the "roaring 20s" in America, the American dream of wealth and happiness, is most certainly attainable. However, Gatsby, after working for money and acceptance in the wealthy community to achieve the love of his life, Daisy, ended up not living his dream. The truth that the American Dream is attainable may not be so universal to everyone, even with determination and love.

> As we have seen from those literary and historical examples, the truth can be deceptive. This is especially important in society today, because in order to grow and prosper, we must look at all the angles and make the necessary changes to fulfill our goal and be ethical.

Alaizah gets off to a rousing start by making up a simple quote that resonates well with her definition of the prompt. She has fun attributing it to Walter Worthington, a fictional character in his own right! Remember, the Readers are specifically instructed **not** to hold content mistakes or historical inaccuracies (in other words, quotes) against you. This is the key to beating the College Board at its own game.

The SAT essay is a treacherous, artificial environment you must master in 25 minutes or less. Fantasy and imagination are the weapons of choice in this SAT duel to the death.

It's a curious thing, but once my students realize that they are not tied by conventional term-paper constraints on the SAT essay, they let their imaginations loose and play with the prompt in ways that the College Board never anticipated.

One of the points of this book is to make essay writing a game. In some sense, the College Board is this huge corporate juggernaut messing unfairly with the prospects for high school kids to get into the college of their choice, so fighting back with a beat-them-at-their-own-game mentality is the attitude I encourage in all my students and the strategy I teach in all my classes.

But I digress. Returning to the essay, notice the contrast Alaizah sets up within her first body paragraph.

> One perspective of this war could have been that America was performing a heroic, admirable deed. However, as New York Journalists, Pulitzer and Hearst, wrote in their newspapers, "you furnish the pictures, we'll furnish the war", the Cubans found our involvement quite selfish and imperialistic.

She uses a nice transition word — however — to turn the beat around, so to speak, and show how the perception of reality changes from an American to a Cuban perspective.

In a later sentence, she brings up the Teller Amendment to lend herself an air of authority and employs a very important trick that all students should pay attention to: she **defines her terms**.

> We established the Teller Amendment (ensuring America's freedom and control in Cuba) and benefited from their economic resources and geographic location.

It's as important in an SAT essay to define your terms as it is to introduce them in the first place. So right after she mentions the Teller Amendment, Alaizah tells the reader what it is. This is the way to score points big time.

She follows up in the next paragraph with the same technique, citing three Anti-bellum amendments and immediately defining each one.

> After we fought for African American rights, we established the 13th, 14th, and 15th amendments. These guaranteed their freedom, voting rights, and laws against discrimination.

Then she wraps up her paragraph by returning to the topic and closing the sale.

> Depending on a Northerner's or an African American (viewpoint), Reconstruction and Civil Rights may or may not have truly served justice to the African Americans in the early 1800s.

In fact, Alaizah neglected to add the word viewpoint — I put it in for her just as the Readers must have, since her context was so clear.

A final example that lack of accuracy is not held against you occurs in Alaizah's last body paragraph, where she attributes *The Great Gatsby* to Hawthorne, rather than F. Scott Fitzgerald.

> Hawthorne's novel *The Great Gatsby*.

A major blunder in a term paper, this is barely a hiccup in an SAT essay. It certainly didn't detract from Alaizah's perfect score. Again, recall that the **SAT Readers are trained to ignore content mistakes AND factual inaccuracies**.

March, 2008 Prompt

Think carefully about the ideas and issues presented in the following excerpt and assignment below.

> Being loyal—faithful or dedicated to someone or something—is not always easy. People often have conflicting loyalties, and there are no guidelines that help them decide to what or whom they should be loyal. Moreover, people are often loyal to something bad. Still, loyalty is one of the essential attributes a person must have and must demand of others.

Assignment: Should people always be loyal? Plan and write an essay in which you develop your point of view on this issue. Support your position with reasoning and examples taken from your reading, studies, experience, or observations.

Loyalty is relatively easy theme to address using the strategies outlined in this book. Carville himself sets the stage for this essay by saying "People often have conflicting loyalties". Conflict, of course, is the bread and butter of all SAT essays, along with drama and its holy trinity: challenges met, obstacles overcome and progress achieved.

Zach H. picks up this ball and runs with it, using F. Scott Fitzgerald in his opening paragraph to show the importance of loyalty under difficult circumstances.

He goes on to use the old standard, Civil Rights, to discuss the importance of loyalty in the context of racial injustice. Then he goes full-lit, focusing on Ishmael in Herman Melville's American masterpiece, *Moby Dick*.

While SAT Readers may be a little tired of kids using Civil Rights in their essays, they stand up and cheer when literary classics are cited. Referencing *Moby Dick* is almost guaranteed to get your score into double digits.

Zach uses a sports example to drive home the importance of loyalty in his own personal experience. As you read his essay, notice how he consistently returns to the theme at the end of each of his body paragraphs. Always be closing.

A nice quote (real or imagined?) from Henry Ford, places the theme of loyalty in sweeping national context in the conclusion.

Zach's Essay (score = 12)

As F. Scott Fitzgerald once said "our happy sense of kinship is a sense of complete fulfilment." In other words, a high loyalty to one's group of friends is central to an enjoyable existence. Fitzgerald, an avid adventurer and wildly successful writer, embodied this notion through his dedicated companionship with his friends and wife, regardless of the situation. As per this example, loyalty to one's companions or peers is vital, no matter how trying the circumstances may be. This notion is exemplified through history, literary works and personal experience.

One exceptional example that loyalty should be unconditional is demonstrated in the Civil Rights Movement. This tremendous example of the unity in the African American Culture began when Rosa Parks valiantly refused to give up her seat to a white man while riding a public bus in 1955. Parks was arrested and jailed for her defiance, but her efforts sparked the

Montgomery Bus Boycott, a movement that lasted for over a year and denied bus companies enormous sums of money. Martin Luther King, Jr., a young activist, was also inspired by Parks' actions. King started hundreds of successful non-violent strikes and demonstrations, including his "I Have a Dream" speech that rallied the efforts of African Americans everywhere. Tragically, King was shot and killed while speaking from a motel in the South. Parks, King, and the entirety of the black population showed tremendous loyalty when faced with severe and often violent opposition, and their efforts resulted in the passage of the 1964 Civil Rights Act.

Another example illustrating loyalty occurs in *Moby Dick*. In the novel, the noble Ishmael boards a ship that will ultimately bring his demise. Captained by the insane Ahab, the Pequod's crew faces unbelievable danger aboard the cursed whaling ship. Ishmael faces a difficult choice because although he knows Ahab's insatiable pursuit of the fabled white whale known as *Moby Dick* will result in the deaths of the entire crew, he feels that his ties to the men on board cannot be severed at any cost. Ishmael keeps his loyalty to the crew even to the bitter end, showing the true importance of loyalty in any situation.

A final illustration of unconditional loyalty is shown in my personal experience involving my first year playing high school football. Our team had tremendous talent, but a lack of unity in the team resulted in numerous losses. Our coaches pushed us very hard, but the chemistry between players simply did not exist. After suffering through the initial portion of the season, players began to give up, a few even left the team. I maintained my loyalty, however, and the remainder of the players did as well. As a result, we crushed the opposing teams in the final chapters of the season, our loyalty carrying us to the victory.

As seen in these numerous examples, loyalty carries unfathomable importance. This holds true particularly in modern times, when the world seems to be in constant conflict. As Henry Ford once said, "Our national pride is what's made this nation great, but that pride doesn't come free."

March, 2009 Prompt

Think carefully about the ideas and issues presented in the following excerpt and assignment below.

> Whatever happened to good manners? Many books and articles have been written about the lack of common courtesy and old-fashioned politeness in today's society. From spoiled children acting out in restaurants to so-called experts yelling at each other on cable news shows, people seem less concerned with good manners and civilized behavior than ever before. On the other hand, if people really want to change the world for the better, they have to risk being seen as impolite or uncivil.

Assignment: Is it sometimes necessary to be impolite? Plan and write an essay in which you develop your point of view on this issue. Support your position with reasoning and examples taken from your reading, studies, experience, or observations.

The importance — or lack thereof — of good manners may seem like a strange topic for an SAT essay. But think about it for a moment. What is the underlying subtext? If you said drama, conflict or tension, well, you've been paying attention. Moreover, you're probably ready to sit down and write a Killer SAT essay.

Which is exactly what Craig D did during the March, 2009 exam.

Craig's Essay (score = 12)

As the noted psychologist Nathan Buers once stated, "Sometimes the most effective path to the solution of a problem involves stepping on a few toes." He is referring to the fact that manners, while a useful part of society, should never get in the way of true progress. All down the tree of history, from the greenest branches to the brownest roots, humankind has had to sidestep social restrictions in order to move forward. I can give evidence of this from personal experience, history and popular culture.

In my own life I have had to force manners to be able to make progress. As a journalist for the school paper, I was assigned to examine why seniors grades were dropping so significantly. I could have just interviewed some seniors, receiving vague and noncommittal answers, but I chose to take it a step further. Immersing myself in the senior party scene, I documented what our schoolmates were really doing after class, creating an insightful study of human behavior in the process. The article earned many of my subject's negative reputations, but I couldn't afford to be polite. The truth had to be told and our school paper won numerous accolades because of it.

Another example of someone naming names in the sake of progress was Jewish guerilla Tzur Reuven. During World War II and the Holocaust, Tzur Reuven's village was deported to ghettoes in Eastern Germany. He and a few young men were able to escape and found refuge in a Soviet military stockade. The Soviets promised to help Reuven and his comrades, but they were going to have to wait for Russia to break the Nazi front. Reuven knew that if he waited patiently like he was asked then his village would be taken to the concentration camps. So he acted decisively, stealing weaponry from the Soviets and escaping to the forests of Northeaster Germany. From there they were able to liberate many of their fellow Jews from tragic death, as well as launch a successful guerilla front from within German borders.

A third instance of progress being made over politeness is music icon David Bowie. In the early 70's Bowie had been pinned down as a folk singer-songwriter. But he wanted to move music forward, no matter what the cost. So he broke relations with his manager and record labels to create the Ziggy Stardust persona, a flamboyant bisexual king of glitter. Bowie could have kept to himself politely, but instead he went out on a limb and risked public opinion, changing the shape of pop music forever.

Progress doesn't wait for us to decide which fork is the proper one to use at which course.

Craig does some fancy footwork in the introduction to his essay, marrying the idea of progress with the need to step on a few toes. This is a classic SAT move that I stress with my students: spin the prompt to include "progress" as part of the topic. This enlarges the scope of the essay, giving the writer more "wiggle room" to bring in content examples that might not otherwise jibe with a strict interpretation of the prompt.

I tell my students that it's not the prompt itself that matters in an SAT essay, it's **YOUR INTERPRETATION OF THE PROMPT** that's crucial. Prompts for a national test are by nature open-ended. It's a mistake to take them too literally, since this invariably paints you into a corner. The secret behind using prefabricated content examples for an SAT essay is knowing how to spin the prompt so that you can put your content examples to use supporting a wide variety of topics.

Craig understands this and uses a motley crew of content examples here: a journalistic expose, an Israeli guerilla (real or imagined?), and David Bowie, glitter king, to support his contention that politeness flies in the face of progress. I particularly like his cryptic conclusion, where he uses an ironic metaphor (table manners) as a counterpoint to the larger-than-life content examples employed in his essay. Way to go, Craig, in a few more years you'll be writing for The Believer.

October, 2010 Prompt

Think carefully about the ideas and issues presented in the following excerpt and assignment below.

> I spent some part of every year at the farm until I was twelve or thirteen years old. The life that I led there was full of charm and so is the memory of it yet. I can call back the faint odors of wildflowers, the sheen of rain-washed foliage, the clatter of raindrops when the wind shook the trees, and the far-off hammering of woodpeckers. I can call back the prairie—and its loneliness and peace.
>
> Adapted from Mark Twain, My Autobiography

Assignment: Is it important for people to spend time outdoors and to learn to appreciate the natural environment? Plan and write an essay in which you develop your point of view on this issue. Support your position with reasoning and examples taken from your reading, studies, experience, or observations.

Ah, the great outdoors. A perfect topic for west coast, tree-hugging liberals! Mike S, an essay-writing veteran with two prior SAT exams under his belt, was so in tune with my system that he didn't even need his prefabricated content examples to ace this prompt. He understood how to grab the Readers attention, pull appropriate content examples out of thin air, mix in quotes and anecdotes, and produce a powerful, interesting, and largely fabricated composition.

Mike's Essay (score = 12)

The Roman orator Cicero once stated, "Ex mei domus est ubi mei vita factavest" or "outside of my home is where my life is made". Cicero understood that most of our lives take place other than inside our homes. The universal notion that spending time outdoors is important can be seen in history, literature and modern media.

An historical illustration of the importance of the outdoors can be seen in the actions of Junipero Serra and the Sierra club. Father Junipero Serra founded the Sierra club for the sole purpose of preserving the great outdoors for future posterity. Serra and his followers fought against deforestation and encroachment on wildlife habitats vocally and even radically. Serra once tied himself to a redwood tree about to be cut down and said, "If you are to cut down this work of God, than you must cut me down." Serra understood the importance of the outdoors and was willing to die to protect it.

Legendary American author Mark Twain is another figure who exemplified the necessity of the great outdoors. Twain wrote many books, fictional and factual, about his experiences outdoors. In his autobiography, he explains that he spent the majority of his childhood outdoors and he says that nature is "full of charm .. . . loneliness and peace." Twain understood the outdoors as a place where one can think clearly, reflect upon the past and gain one's composure. Mark twain later states in his autobiography that "without having spent much time outdoors, in the woods and steams and prairies, I would be most unhappy."

The importance of nature is also portrayed in the modern media. The Discovery Channel program "Planet Earth" is a portrait of the vast and varying expanses of wilderness on our planet. The program shows wildlife in a natural environment undisturbed by mankind, living to the full potential of its beauty. The T.V. series hits home, for today's society, how important our planet's un-humanized side is, because without it, we would have nothing.

The universal notion of the importance of the outdoors is illustrated throughout history, literature and modern media. Junipero Serra, Mark Twain, and Discovery Channel's "Planet Earth" all prove that the outdoors is paramount to not just our survival but earth's as well. As Spanish historian Santayana once said, "The Earth is all we have, we might as well use what we've got, the way it is, and protect it with all we've got."

First off, to impress the Readers with his erudition, Mike **made up a quote in Latin**, which he attributed to — who else? — Cicero. Then he translated the quote into English, giving it even greater purchase and employing it as a perfect segue to his topic sentence. Outstanding.

As a righteous California boy, he created an entirely imaginary coalition between Father Junipero Serra and — could you believe it? — the Sierra Club to rail against the evils of deforestation. No problem that these two entities happened to exist about 300 years apart; it's the thought (and writing style) that counts.

His paragraph on Mark Twain employs Tara's strategy (April, 2006) to mine the quote box from the prompt as a source of content material for the essay. Beautiful.

Finally, he brings in modern media (the Discovery Channel) to buttress his argument that the natural environment must be preserved and appreciated. Perfect.

His conclusion simply recapitulates the content examples discussed in his essay and throws one final bone to the Readers by quoting (imaginatively, to be sure) the Spanish philosopher Santayana, whom he'd read about in Chapter 6 (Quotes) of my book.

He did all this **on the fly** because he was steeped in the strategies and techniques he learned in my class.

Once you understand how to mix and match the component parts of an SAT essay, how to use quotes, how to insert anecdotes, how to devise prefabricated content, how to spin prompts, and, finally, how to make stuff up! — once you understand all that, man, like a jazz musician or a hip-hop dancer you are free to improvise, free to let your spirit soar, free to **WRITE**.

Less Than Perfect

One final word. All the essays presented in this chapter received a perfect score of 12. It should be noted that a 12 is very difficult score to obtain, given the *wholistic* subjectivity with which the Readers judge an essay's worth.

Consequently, in later chapters I present a number of essays that received a score of 11, a more realistic and easily-attainable goal. I've had many students who scored an 8 the first time around in their essays and, after taking my program, received an 11. So take heart, the principles I'm presenting here are not just for top writers; my students *average* a score of 10, and over 30% receive 11s or 12s.

6—Quotes

≡

Snappy quotes relevant to the topic at hand spice up an essay and lend authority and credence to the exposition. Practicing what I preach, I've made liberal use of quotes myself in this book. Here's a sampling of some of the sayings included so far:

> All animals are created equal, but some animals are more equal than others (George Orwell)

> The ideas of one generation become the instincts of the next. (D. H. Lawrence)

> Whatever doesn't kill me makes me stronger. (Friederich Nietzche)

> So we beat on, boats against the current, borne back ceaselessly into the past. (F. Scott Fitzgerald)

> You may be disappointed if you fail, but you are doomed if you don't try. (Beverly Sills)

> Imagination is more important than knowledge. (Einstein)

> If I have seen further it is by standing on the shoulders of Giants. (Sir Isaac Newton)

In this chapter, I'm going to provide you with a list of famous quotes you can use for your essays. Associated with each quote, I'll include a paragraph showing you how one of my students used the quote to good effect in his or her sample essay in my class. To give the paragraph context, I'll include an abbreviated version of the prompt that inspired it.

First, here's a listing of all the famous quotes used in this chapter.

List of Famous Quotes

> Those who fail to understand the past are forever forced to repeat it — Santayana
> You can't judge a book by its cover — anonymous
> You know the world's messed up when the best golfer is a black guy and the best rapper is a white guy — Charles Barkley
> Beauty is in the eye of the beholder — anonymous

Whatever can go wrong, will go wrong — Murphy's Law
If at first you don't succeed, try, try again — anonymous
No pain, no gain — anonymous
Of mankind in general, the parts are greater than the whole — Aristotle
The road to hell is paved with good intentions — Dante
The only thing we have to fear is fear itself — Franklin Delano Roosevelt

Famous Quotes in Context

- *Those who fail to understand the past are forever forced to repeat it* — Santayana
  Prompt: Are heroes important to modern society?
  Paragraph (by Lindsey C.): The Spanish historian Santayana once said, "Those who refuse to understand the past will be forced to repeat it." Throughout history and literature we can learn how to improve ourselves by looking at the mistakes and positive actions that others, especially heroes, have made. This universal notion is exemplified throughout history and literature.

- *You can't judge a book by its cover* — anonymous
  Prompt: Are appearances deceptive?
  Paragraph (by Ali K.): The timeless adage, "Do not judge a book by its cover," suggests that things are not always what they seem. Appearances can be deceptive and oversimplified, while the surface of an issue, object, or person often masks a deeper truth. Throughout history, literature, and science, the reality is often more complicated than a first glance provides.

- *You know the world's messed up when the best golfer is a black guy and the best rapper is a white guy* — Charles Barkley
  Prompt: Are appearances deceptive?
  Paragraph (by Lindsey J.): As we have seen in these historical and literary examples, appearances are often deceptive. Despite the awareness of this issue, many continue to fall for beauty, luxury, and mystery without any concern for true identity. Charles Barkley shows his belief for this theory claiming "You know the world's messed up when the best golfer is a black guy and the best rapper is a white guy."

- *Beauty is in the eye of the beholder* —anonymous
  Prompt: Are appearances deceptive?
  Paragraph (by Katie B.): A common adage pertaining to appearance proclaims "beauty is in the eye of the beholder." In this case, beauty is not necessarily relating to aesthetics, but simply the way something looks or what makes it different or special. Nevertheless, this elementary proverb is undeniably true. Everyone looks at things differently which makes appearances very deceptive. This universal truth is exemplified throughout history and literature.

- *Of mankind in general, the parts are greater than the whole* — Aristotle
  Prompt: Are individuals more important than the group?

Paragraph (by Maddy R.): As Aristotle once said, "Of mankind in general, the parts are greater than the whole." Often, in an argument, pleasing both sides is just not an option because sometimes the needs of the individual outweighs the need of the majority. It is proven throughout history, and my personal experience that in times of uncertainty, the desires of one person outweigh the desires of the group.

- *The road to hell is paved with good intentions* — Dante
  Prompt: Do actions speak louder than words?
  Paragraph (by Sean S.): The theme that actions speak louder than words is demonstrated in the historical events which led up to the American Revolutionary War. For numerous decades the Anglo-American colonists, still loyal to King George of England, sought to talk about their problems with the multitude of taxes they thought were unfair. Parliament, however, would not budge. The Colonists did not act upon their instincts to stand up against England because they wanted to maintain a healthy relationship. The colonists soon realized, like Dante once said, "the road to hell is paved with good intentions." Although the colonists had good intentions such as maintaining peace and attempting to forge ahead as one unified country, America was failing economically and many immigrants to the country were struggling more than before the new taxes. Colonists eventually realized that they were on a destructive path and began to change their ways. They fought for their rights as an individual country and, in time, won their liberty from England's oppressive government.

- *Whatever can go wrong, will go wrong* — Murphy's Law
  Prompt: Do the best laid plans of mice and men often go awry?
  Paragraph (by Kent H.): Murphy's Law states that, "Whatever can go wrong will go wrong." Too often we, as humans, find ourselves believing that we have planned so carefully as to have eliminated the possibility of something going awry. However, the reality is that no matter how much effort we put into our plans, many things can still go wrong. This universal notion is exemplified throughout modern literature, history, and my personal experiences.

- *If at first you don't succeed, try, try again* — anonymous
  Prompt: No progress is possible without sacrifice.
  Paragraph (Angelika L.): A famous saying states that "if at first you don't succeed, try, then try again". This profound advice suggests that failure is inevitable before success. The notion that obstacles must be overcome in order to progress is exemplified throughout science, international politics and America's new approach to a healthy lifestyle.

- *No pain, no gain* and *If at first you don't succeed, try, try again* — anonymous
  Prompt: No progress is possible without sacrifice.

Paragraph (Noelle P.): Even our most carefully planned projects can have something go wrong with them. Most people in the world would agree that no progress is possible without sacrifice. A famous proverb says: "If at first you don't succeed, try, try again." This profound advice suggests that failure is inevitable before success. Another common adage says: "No pain, no gain." In other words, success results from hard work. This universal notion is exemplified throughout history, literature and technology.

- *The only thing we have to fear is fear itself* — FDR
  Prompt: No progress is possible without sacrifice.
  Paragraph (by Kaitlin S.): Franklin Delano Roosevelt once said, "The only thing we have to fear is fear itself." Society is constantly striving to improve itself and if fear of the unexpected ever got in the way, we would never accomplish our goals. Things go wrong and mistakes are made, but it is necessary to take risks in order to actualize dreams. The universal notion that no progress is possible without fault is exemplified throughout history and literature.

- *Fate had other plans in store for me; I listened and learned and then let be.* — Robert Frost
  Prompt: Do the best laid plans often go awry?
  Paragraph (by Hillary M.): As seen in these examples of literature, technology, and personal experience, careful planning cannot always prevail over unpredictable occurrences. However, we must keep in mind that although our plans may not go our way, we still take away new understanding from the experience. As the poet Robert Frost once wrote, "Fate had other plans in store for me; I listened and learned and then let be."

So there you have it. Some good quotes put to good use in some sample essays.

But wait, you say, this last one wasn't actually on the list. Hmm, come to think of it, you're right. Well, where did it come from?

Hillary must have made it up to sound like Robert Frost and conclude her essay with a poetic flourish. Even rhymed it in a style reminiscent of the author. Fooled me when I first read it. You too, apparently. Like I've been saying: imagination is more important than knowledge.

7—Details, Details, Details

As everyone knows, the devil is always in the details. Bad writing is vague, unmemorable and abstract. For example, compare this: I took a plane to Hawaii for a vacation on the beach. To this: I bought a first-class ticket on Hawaiian Airlines for a trip to the Big Island, where we stayed in a secluded condominium on the beach, surrounded by surf and sand, our only neighbors a few wild goats and the occasional Monk Seal lounging in the shallows nearby. The first example is vague, unmemorable and abstract. The second leaves a more vivid (if somewhat florid) impression.

To some extent, writing is like painting. On the SAT essay, the more color, the more brush strokes, the better. Remember, readers will only take at most a couple of minutes evaluating your essay. To obtain a top score, you have to make an impression.

To that end, this chapter presents a collection of vivid content examples from a wide range of categories, everything from history to pop culture to technology.

Rather than a sit-down dinner, this chapter is a buffet-style Sunday brunch. There's something here for everyone: french toast, eggs benedict, smoked salmon, caesar salad. Of course, you're not going to want to sample everything all at once. Walk the room with a plate and try a little here, try a little there. Survey the surroundings. Stop and smell the roses. Most of all, pace yourself — too much food (for thought) is not necessarily a good thing. Come back periodically for a taste.

Arranged before you is a collection of individual paragraphs (content examples) composed by my SAT students over the past few years. I've organized them into different categories so that you can focus on one group at a time.

≡
_____

As I pointed out way back in the beginning of this book, I'm a strong advocate of learning by doing. So study these examples, re-write them in your own words, borrow snappy phrases left and right, pay attention to sentence structure (particularly subordination), pick up on new vocabulary, and make a mental note of dates and **details**. In short, absorb and incorporate these sample paragraphs into your own individual Bag of Tricks. Soon enough you'll be a writer in your own write.

The content examples provided here support a variety of prompts, many of which deal with creativity, the mother of all prompts, as I'll point out in the next chapter. Other prompts will be clear from the context. The paragraphs are organized by category and include the following:

- Literature
- Movies
- Music
- Sports
- Art
- Technology
- History
- Personal Experience

Note: I split Popular Culture up into its most prominent sub-categories (movies, music, sports and art) for easy access. Also note that these paragraphs, like all the writing from my students in this book, is presented "as is". I've intentionally avoided "botoxing" any prose wrinkles so that what you see is exactly what I got.

Literature

In this section, the following novels are employed by student writers in content examples to support various topics:

- Scarlet Letter
- Grapes of Wrath
- Odyssey
- Crucible
- 1984
- One Flew Over the Cuckoo's Nest
- Great Gatsby
- Huck Finn
- Walt Whitman
- To Kill a Mockingbird
- Lord of the Rings (LOTR)

- Dr. Jekyll and Mr. Hyde
- Catcher in the Rye
- As I Lay Dying
- Antigone
- Brave New World
- Romeo and Juliet
- Thus Spake Zarathustra
- Ender's Game

The Scarlet Letter

Katie B — A final illustration that one must not rely on appearance for an objective analysis is found in the classic novel *The Scarlet Letter*. This tale of adultery follows the protagonist, Hester Prynne, who must bare a letter "A" on her clothing to make all the townspeople aware of her sins. The townspeople all look down on her and create an opinion of her based solely on her promiscuous act. No one bothers to look beyond the 'A' and see the virtuous, charitable women inside. On the other end of the spectrum, the Reverend Dimmsdale, Hester's partner in the act, maintains his righteous image to the town, but is internally racked by his guilt and shame.

Comments: This is an excellent analysis of the major themes of the book and clearly supports the topic. It shows sophisticated use of language and exhibits excellent transitions. I particularly like the last sentence where Katie analyzes Rev Dimmsdale's psychological state, saying he is "internally racked by his guilt and shame".

Grapes of Wrath

Nick B — A final illustration that the best plans are at the mercy of chance events occurs in John Steinbeck's novel, *The Grapes of Wrath*. The Joad family, as a specific example, and the majority of the farming population in Oklahoma as a wider representation, are driven from their land by drought and the Dust Bowl and forced to move West in search of work and a new life. Upon reaching California, they find there are hordes of applicants for every job, and thus, little hope of finding a stable income from which to live, let alone find a house and a steady job. In Steinbeck's work, it is the reality of life, versus the Joad's preconceived fantasies of life as a migrant worker in California, that serves as the unexpected element in the Joad's seemingly flawless plan.þ

Comments: Good writing, although the sentence structure seems to wobble a bit. Nice vocab ("hordes of applicants"), good transitions and good support for the topic.

≡

Rob G — John Steinbeck's masterpiece, *The Grapes of Wrath*, is one of the greatest examples of plans going awry. The Joad family leaves their home with a simple plan: make their way to beautiful California where jobs are plentiful and peaches can be plucked from every tree and savored as the juice runs down one's neck. Rather than sit back passively in the Dust Bowl, the Joads as a family make plans to move West. On their journey, the family encounters many hardships, but these are only a taste of what is yet to come. Upon reaching California, the family becomes broke, working for nickels to provide that night's dinner. The perfect plan of having a great life in California has turned completely around and now the Joads seem doomed.

Comments: This is a very colorful depiction of the Dust Bowl era in general and the Joad family in particular. Rob uses nice transitions and stays tightly focused on the topic, plans gone wrong. An excellent paragraph.

Odyssey

Mark C — Literature is a powerful agent for progress. By reading the stories of how innovative goals help characters in books, people can transfer that to their lives Creativity as a way to set and achieve goals is prevalent in *The Odyssey*. Odysseus, the protagonist of the epic poem, has as his paramount goal to get home, but he has mammoth obstacles. Never losing sight of his goal, Odysseus uses his creative mind to get himself out of dangerous situations. Cleverly, he escapes Scylla, the six headed monster, Charbdis, a dangerous whirlpool, and the deadly irresistible Sirens. Probably Odysseus makes the most progress towards his goal by cunningly escaping the Cyclopes, Polyphemus. Trapped in the giant's cave, Odysseus gets Polyphemus drunk and tells him that his name is "Nobody." When Odysseus stabs the Cyclopes in the eye and the other Cyclopes comes to help, Polyphemus shouts, "Nobody is killing me." Thinking he is not in danger the other Cyclopes go away. Odysseus then escapes by clinging to a sheep's belly as it walks out of the cave. With Odysseus' never-ending determination to reach his goal, he survives and returns home.

Comments: Extremely detailed and fluid description of Odysseus' encounter with the Cyclops, including this wonderful line: "Odysseus then escapes by clinging to a sheep's belly as it walks out of the cave." If we're talking detail, this is the way to go. Mark also brings in Scylla, the six headed monster, and Charbdis to give the essay depth. Excellent narrative synopsis.

Crucible

Rachel H — The quintessential example of a majority opinion being a poor guide is in Arthur Millers *The Crucible*. In the book, there was no character that was able to stand up against the majority opinion, in an attempt to infuse another perspective on the situation. The Salem society was so absorbed with one idea of the truth, that no one was able to break free. In the small Puritan town of Salem, Massachusetts a witch trial is born on the foundation of a young girls lie. The township spirals out of control with persecutions and dooms innocent men and women. The town is so consumed by the majority opinion that they are unable to see truths until it is too late. Small communities like in *The Crucible* often act like cults against a common enemy. Once one person jumped to accusations, the rest of the town followed. In *The Crucible*, the opinion of the majority ends up being a poor path to follow, and sets off a chain reaction of persecutions across New England.

Comments: Nice vocab ("quintessential example") to get the paragraph started. Nice phrasing ("spirals out of control") and excellent analysis of the play in the larger context of society ("Small communities like in *The Crucible* often act like cults against a common enemy.").

1984

Padon S — One example of the popular opinion as a poor guide is George Orwell's *1984*. In this novel, everyone is being watched and controlled by Big Brother. Big Brother's government is very oppressive and tries to eliminate all chances of rebellion. They are even creating a new language called newspeak that eliminates all words that could threaten the government's power. The main character, Winston Smith, starts to resent Big Brother and he starts to rebel by writing in a diary and getting a girlfriend. These actions would not be looked down upon in the real world, but in this novel they are very illegal. Eventually, Winston gets caught doing these very illegal things and is taught to love Big Brother again. In this case, the opinion of the majority is obviously a poor guide as it prohibits humans from any kind of individuality or freedom. Although Winston's rebellion against the opinion of the majority does not make any difference in his world, it was important for him to rebel in order to show just how poor a guide the majority's opinion is.

Comments: A good, straightforward plot summary of the book with excellent transitions.

One Flew over the Cuckoo's Nest

Dina K — One compelling illustration that progress is impossible without sacrifice is demonstrated in Ken Kesey's novel, *One Flew Over the Cuckoo's Nest*. In this novel, which takes place in a psychiatric hospital, the dictatorial Nurse Ratched, controls and treats the patients unfairly. When a new patient Randle McMurphy attends the hospital, he rebels against Nurse Ratched's suppressive power. McMurphy inspires the patients to gain more confidence, and to demand better treatment. However, this achievement of power is not met without sacrifice as McMurphy receives a lobotomy as punishment for his rebellion.

Comments: Good, straightforward and uncluttered description of the novel. Excellent support for the topic. I particularly like the sentence where Dina introduces Nurse Ratched: "In this novel, which takes place in a psychiatric hospital, the dictatorial Nurse Ratched, controls and treats the patients unfairly." Nice use of the word "dictatorial".

The Great Gatsby

Lindsey C — The theme that loss accompanies gain can also be seen in *The Great Gatsby* by F. Scott Fitzgerald. Gatsby, the protagonist of the novel, recreates his whole image to gain his sweet heart, Daisy. He is able to turn himself from rags to rich by selling and trading on the black market. He lives in a mansion, has a numerous amount of cars, and throws tremendous parties, yet Gatsby is sad inside because he only has materialistic gain. He forgets who he really is in the process of transforming himself into a rich man. As a tragic hero, Gatsby is a great example of the sacrifice that comes along with progress.

Comments: Although the writing is a little unfocused, the psychological insight into Gatsby's materialistic take on life — and his consequent loss of identity — is excellent.

Huck Finn

Alaizah K — The theme that sacrifice is necessary for goals to be obtained occurs in Mark Twain's classic novel *The Adventures of Huckleberry Finn*. Huck Finn, a carefree, compassionate young adult, befriends a runaway slave and assists him in his quest for freedom. The two companions begin their journey traveling down the Mississippi River, in search of a free state. Although Huck enjoyed his thrilling adventure, he was forced to leave the security of his home and risk punishment or even death for illegally leading Jim to a free state. It was not only necessary, but also heroic of Huck to take those risks and make such sacrifices for the sake of his friend's happiness.

Comments: Good plot summary and nice support for the topic. Excellent character description as in "Huck Finn, a carefree, compassionate young adult, befriends a runaway slave and assists him in his quest for freedom."

Clay S — The protagonist of Mark Twain's American classic, *The Adventures of Huckleberry Finn*, is able to rebel against the confines of the South's racist society through his ingenuity and individuality. Huck, while adopted into a prosperous family and given educational opportunities, eschews the limitations society places on his freedom. Escaping from home by floating down the Mississippi River on a raft, Huck challenges the expectations that one must conform to established lifestyles. Furthermore, Huck helps liberate a runaway slave, Jim, while on his trek. While conflicted over whether to help

Jim because of the pressures of racial prejudices in his contemporary South, Huck nevertheless devotes himself to saving the good-natured slave. Huck refutes the racial superiority of whites and the accepted religious justifications for slavery in saving Jim, demonstrating that Huck's magnanimity allows him to transcend widely-held unjust beliefs.

Comments: Impressive vocabulary ("eschews the limitations society places on his freedom") and powerful concluding sentence.

Walt Whitman

Clay S — Another example of the importance of originality is American poet Walt Whitman, whose innovative appreciation for nature, the human body, and patriotism contributed to his place as America's preeminent poet. Living during the 1800s, Whitman wrote several volumes of poems in which he expressed his respect for the beauty and spontaneity of nature. His use of free verse and audacious imagery invoked the ire of traditionalist poets; Whitman challenged the very concept of what poetry was. His famous poems "I hear America Sing", "The Brooklyn Ferry", and his collection "Leaves of Grass" adulate the diversity of the American population and the beautiful uniqueness of the individual. Walt Whitman's fearless divergence from accepted poetic styles and topics show his originality.

Comments: Two in a row from Clay, who continues to use impressive vocabulary and phrasing -- "His use of free verse and audacious imagery invoked the ire of traditionalist poets". Notice also how Clay makes reference to specific works of Whitman to impress the Readers with concrete detail.

To Kill a Mockingbird

David D — A final illustration that shows the importance of overcoming obstacles or unexpected events occurs in Harper Lee's, *To Kill a Mockingbird*. The protagonist, Atticus Finch, is a lawyer representing an innocent black man, Tom Robinson. The racist town in Alabama does not want to believe that a black man is innocent, but Atticus is determined to give his client justice. The idea of a white man defending a black man causes Atticus to be shunned from Macon County and perceived as an outcast. Despite these difficult times, Atticus is able to rise above the town's hatred to seek justice for Tom Robinson.

Comments: Good plot summary with nice support for the topic. Interesting use of vocabulary with "shunned" "protagonist" and "perceived as an outcast."

Lord of the Rings

Griffin B — Literature has also had a profound impact on expressing ethical behavior, as demonstrated in J.R.R Tolkien's fantasy novel *The Lord of the Rings*. In the novel, Frodo inherits a ring of great power from his uncle Bilbo and must embark on a perilous quest to destroy it before it falls into the hands of great evil forces headed by the fearsome Sauron. In his quest to destroy the one ring to rule them all, Frodo realizes that the burden is one that he must conquer on his own. Although aided by many a heroic friend, including the great wizard Gandalf and Aragorn, the king of men, the psychological burden and lust for the ring that Frodo develops is a lonely battle that he must face. After many years of fearsome battle and a deteriorating hope for success, Frodo overcomes the odds and destroys the ring. Frodo's significant accomplishment saved middle earth from imminent death and suffering of the dark forces, thus emphasizing the effect ethical behavior in the name of good can have on the whole of society.

Comments: Great encapsulation of story and detail. Excellent phrasing: "must embark on a perilous quest" and later "the psychological burden and lust for the ring" This paragraph does a great job of capturing the loneliness of Frodo's quest and the social implications of his success.

Dr. Jekyll and Mr. Hyde

Katie O — Another credible example of the idea that even the best laid plans are at the mercy of the unknown is exemplified through the novel by Robert Louis Stevenson, *Dr. Jekyll and Mr. Hyde*. The protagonist, Dr. Jekyll, began his experiment with the best of intentions and an almost perfect plan; to separate the common person's good and evil side, and possibly create a perfect society. Jekyll began his experiments on the only person he was willing to sacrifice if needed, himself. However, in the end his evil side dominated and eventually contributed to his death. Although Jekyll had carefully planned his experiment, in the end he could no longer control what he had created and his plans simply went to the mercy of the unknown.

Comments: This paragraph does a very good job of highlighting the contrast between good and evil that is at the heart of Stevenson's novel. Good sentence variety and transitions.

Catcher in the Rye

Andrew P — Another person who viewed the majority as a poor guide is Holden Caulfield from the novel *Catcher in the Rye*. Holden is a rebellious young man who is determined to see his own ideals and thoughts carried out. Throughout the novel, he constantly opposes the public opinion of conformity and seeks his own path of individualism. This individualism stems from his endless imagination and unblocked freedom of thought. It is Holden's commitment to follow himself as a guide that allows him to be truly unique, not just another number in the majority. Holden sees how joining the majority strips people of their own ability to think for themselves and function as individuals. If one joins the group, that person loses their freedom as an individual. Thus, Holden beats down the temptations to follow the majority and thinks freely for himself, allowing Holden to make choices that most benefit himself.

Comments: I like the way Andrew hones in on the key point of Holden Caulfield's sensibility: "Holden sees how joining the majority strips people of their own ability to think for themselves and function as individuals." Excellent analysis.

As I Lay Dying

Nathan B — In his award-winning novel "As I Lay Dying", William Faulkner tells the tragic story of the Bundrens, a Southern family who must travel across Mississippi to bury their recently deceased wife and mother, Addie. Unfortunately, they meet a multitude of obstacles, both physical and psychological, along the way. Due to the different personalities and philosophies of each member of the family, they find themselves in constant disagreement and unable to work together. Thus, a family that should be united in the wake of their matriarch's death drifts even farther apart than they were while she was still alive.

Comments: Excellent transitions, sentence structure and vocab: "Unfortunately, they meet a multitude of obstacles, both physical and psychological, along the way." Nathan handles this paragraph with a writing style that Faulkner would have been proud of.

Antigone

Julia W — The importance of fostering different and novel ideas is also demonstrated through Sophocles' play, *Antigone*. The protagonist, Antigone, sees the importance of burying her brother Polynices, because the gods will everyone a proper burial. Antigone believes it unfair that her father, Creon, decides who has the right to be honored in death, and sneaks away to bury her brother against Creon's wishes. If Antigone never stuck up for her beliefs, armed with her new way of thinking for equality, her brother would have been disgraced in both the human and underworlds. Although Antigone ends tragically, with 3 suicides, Creon learns that Antigone was brave and pure hearted; he must live with the guilt of causing his whole family's destruction. Antigone's willingness to think differently was vital to save her brother's honor and dignity.

Comments: Using a classic Greek tragedy as a content example is a sure way to impress the readers. Moreover, Julia's plot summary is right on the money and her spin -- that Antigone was thinking outside the box -- is perfect. Nice job.

Brave New World

Kendall W — The theme that unexpected events often change even our best plans also occurs in Aldous Huxley's novel, *Brave New World*. The novel explores a utopian city inhabited by well-trained citizens. Each citizen must undergo social conditioning by means of hypnopaedia, or sleep-teaching, oxygen deprivation, and shock therapy in order to guarantee a "perfect" city. Yet, due to the fact that achieving a problem-free town is unattainable, chaos erupts in the city upon the unexpected arrival of a man who has not taken part in any conditioning. He, unlike the other members of the community, is able to form his own opinions and think thoughts different from those around him. His visit sparks the genesis of new ideas among the citizens and thus, their city is forever altered.

Comments: This paragraph gets straight to the point: "The novel explores a utopian city inhabited by well-trained citizens." Excellent transitions, vocab and parallel structure. Kendall's writing style is elegant and the sentence structure varied.

Romeo and Juliet

Jess C— Another example of imagination being crucial to creating progress in society can be seen in Shakespeare's play *Romeo and Juliet*. This heartbreaking tragedy exemplifies the passionate dominance that love can hold over lovers, and the measures that two people will go to in order to fuel their love. Romeo and Juliet use creative schemes to hide their romance from their quarreling families. In the end, fate conspires against the young couple, but the legacy of their love lives on and unites their families. Without creativity, the "star crossed lovers" would not have been able to keep their secret relationship ignited.

Comments: Using Shakespeare is another sure-fire way to impress the readers. I really liked the way Jess sums up the tragedy with this line: "In the end, fate conspires against the young couple, but the legacy of their love lives on and unites their families." Beautiful.

Thus Spake Zarathustra

Grace M — Moreover, the existential views of Friedrich Nietzche, though radically different from that of Emerson, also stresses the role of individual thinking. In his work, "Thus Spake Zarathustra" Nietzsche warns that the tradition of western society has mechanized human living. Only selected men can overcome social mores and discover peace in life. These "Ubermanches" or supermen, can accept the meaninglessness of life and find ultimate satisfaction by acting according to their own instincts. Therefore, men who do not follow tradition, who rely on themselves for original ideas, will not be absorbed into the absurdities of modern life. According to Nietzche, the ideal life in this meaningless world involves a rejection of tradition. And like Emerson, the radical ideas of Nietzche spawned the existential movement, which gave a generation of post-WWII intellects some solace and explanation for the brutal reality. Men with new ideas can have more power to sway minds than the toughest acts of coercion.

Comments: All you can do is sit back and marvel at the intelligence, style, historical sweep and philosophical depth of this paragraph. Hard to believe that Grace was only a junior in high school when she wrote this. By now, she's probably sipping wine at a cafe neaer the Sorbonne, catching up on the collected works of Jacques Lacan or deconstructing Derrida.

Enders Game

Eric K — Finally, creativity is vital to Ender Wiggin, the protagonist in Orson Scott Card's novel "Ender's Game." Ender Wiggin is a brilliant child who is taken from his home on earth and sent to Battle School: a military training facility in space. The school revolves around a "game" where child soldiers are assembled into armies and fight mock battles to learn military strategy; and Ender is the best. There, he sharpens his already strategic mind to think like his enemy, exploit his weakness and destroy him. Although he earns his commander status years early, he creates new tactics, unprecedented before in the history of the game. Ender's creativity allows him to overcome incredible obstacles and save mankind. In the end, he saves humanity from being exterminated by alien "buggers."

Comments: Not exactly "classic literature" but nonetheless a great novel for teenage boys. Hey, girls have Stephanie Meyers (see *Twilight* in the Movie section below) so it's only fair to include something action-oriented and appropriately low-brow here for the guys. Besides, how can you resist a concluding sentence that reads: "In the end, he saves humanity from being exterminated by alien 'buggers.'" Enough said.

Movies

In this section, the following American movies are employed by student writers in content examples to support various topics:

- Twilight
- Legally Blond
- Spiderman

- Shrek
- Peter Pan
- Toy Story
- Iron Man
- Ratatouille
- Avatar
- The Dark Knight

Twilight

Megan T — The author of the *Twilight* series, Stephanie Meyer, changed the world with her vampire-werewolf-books. She was able to expand a short dream she had from a simple scene of man and a woman in a romantic meadow setting into three novels of a storyline filled with a forbidden love that has captured the attention of millions of teens and even whole families in the world today. Stephanie introduced to the world a vampire sensation, in which teens now all dream of finding a perfect vampire boyfriend who has lived for a hundred years. Her creative mind concocted a story that brought about many more vampire books produced, movies made, and T.V. shows run. Stephanie brought about a near obsession into the world, of vampires, which would not have begun without the creativity she used to concoct the story in the first place.

Comments: Megan hits the nail on the head when she describes the attraction *Twilight* has for teenage girls as a "storyline filled with a forbidden love".

Legally Blonde

Meghan S — Another woman who fought for a new lifestyle can be found in the movie *Legally Blonde*. Reese Witherspoon plays a girl initially trying to get her boyfriend back. She creatively comes up with the plan to get into the college he is enrolled in. Although she is considered no more than an unsophisticated party girl she decides to prove everyone wrong. Through hard work, "Elle" gets into Harvard, evidence that she can do whatever she puts her mind to. She transforms into a hard-working law student at Harvard, amazing her peers, her ex-boyfriend among them. In the end Elle emerges as an independent girl, obtaining more than just the boyfriend she was after. Elle becomes a mature woman working hard in her field of law and fighting for what she believes in.

Comments: Meghan employs *Legally Blonde* to showcase women's independence. Nice writing style with a good subordination and sentence variety.

Spiderman

Chris T — Every film involving a super hero supports the idea heroes are needed in society today. In 2001 the first *Spiderman* was released to the public. Spiderman, "your regular teenage nerd," after being bitten by a radioactive spider, gains super human powers and commences in protecting his city of Chicago. Almost instantly he becomes a hit, and while he is around, the citizens of Chicago feel safe. As in all actions movies though, the protagonist has to overcome a behemoth of an opponent. When society sees Spiderman fail against his opponent, the green goblin, at first, one and all loses faith and the whole city begins to crumble. Evidently, "Spidey" finds the strength to beat the opponent and the whole city is able to operate again. Heroes are not always of the large scale of *Spiderman*, some have a more substantial effect on the individual rather than Society as a whole.

Comments: Good plot summary of the film, nice vocab ("behemoth of an opponent") and excellent conclusion, giving a personal twist to the story.

Shrek

Anne H — Another instance where a character transforms due to the effects of social interactions is in the movie "Shrek." Shrek is an ogre and nobody will take a chance to get to know him. Because of this isolation from the community Shrek becomes scornful and hateful of other people. Shrek is sent on a journey to rescue Princess Fiona and he is accompanied by Donkey. Donkey is a key component to Shrek's transformation into a caring and accepting being. He teaches Shrek that "Ogres are like onions, they have layers." Like an onion, Shrek has built up a tough skin to keep people out of his life, but over time, as he sheds the rough layers and opens up to people, it is clear that Shrek is kind. Without Donkey's help Shrek never would have come to understand that he can be an accepted member of society -- he just needs to show people that he isn't dangerous.

Comments: Anne sums up the sociological aspects of the film in her first sentence where she describes Shrek as a character who "transforms due to the effects of social interactions". Her analysis of the role the Donkey plays in Shrek's transformation is spot on.

Peter Pan

Jac G — Finally, there is also occurrence of creative thinking in Disney's classic children's film, *Peter Pan*. Peter Pan is a young boy who never wants to grow up. He visits the Darling family in London to listen to their daughter Wendy, tell stories. One night, Wendy and her two brothers decide to fly to Never Land, Peter's hometown and a place where nobody ever grows up. Once there, the children are faced with danger and although Peter bravely rescues his friend Tiger Lily from the infamous Captain Hook , the real brave thinker in this story is Wendy. She has the choice to stay in Never Land forever, with her new friends and love interest Peter and never have to grow old. However, she decides to go back to London to be with her family and become a young lady. This brave act concludes the story with the message that although being a kid is fun, there are so many rewards of being an adult and Wendy recognizes this when she makes her choice. No one ever really wants to grow up, to take on new responsibilities and to act in a proper manner, however through Wendy's creative decision, she finds new happiness in her life and shows that alternative solutions can have positive results.

Comments: Excellent encapsulation by Jac of the dilemma at the heart of *Peter Pan*: staying young in Never Land or taking on the responsibilities of adulthood. Excellent take on the tradeoffs involved in making a choice.

Toy Story

Ryan A — Using creativity to solve difficult problems has always been such a familiar theme in our society, that it is often worked into the plots of various novels and films. One example of this is in the recent film *Toy Story 3*. Woody has to rescue Buzz and all his friends from a daycare center, where they are held against their will by Lotso-Huggin Bear, whose purple, plush exterior and southern drawl hide a far more sinister disposition. Woody concocts an elaborate escape plan, which involves using different toys as diversions to distract Lotsos guards. Through his creative thinking, Woody is able to break everyone out of the daycare center and return to his owner.

Comments: Really nice plot summary of the film. You don't always have to come up with brilliant insight into character and theme. Sometimes a simple summary is sufficient. Remember, one of the main criteria for obtaining a high essay score is length. In other words, *keep the pencil moving*.

Iron Man

Nicole T — The notion that imaginative figures are needed in society is depicted in the recent film "Iron Man". Tony Stark, after being held captive by terrorists, decides to eschew his former life of inventing weapons of destruction, donning a near-indestructible suit of armor and becoming the hero Iron Man. Although he faces resentment from a majority of society, Stark continues to express his originality by protecting people from terrorists, sacrificing his personal life and himself. Stark realized that his weapons weren't benefiting the world as much as he thought they could, and in knowing so, he decides to use his creative intellect for the greater good and become a masked hero. Through his self-sacrifice, Tony Stark proves to society that the good shall succeed and that creativity is needed in the world. Even if the people do not know Iron Man's significance in the world, he continues to stand as a creative individual.

Comments: Nice to sprinkle some flash vocab and stylish sentence structure in your essay as Nicole does here in the following description: "Tony Stark, after being held captive by terrorists, decides to eschew his former life of inventing weapons of destruction, donning on a near-indestructible suit of armor and becoming the hero Iron Man."

Ratatouille

Kurt M — Through the medium of film, *Ratatouille* sends the message that breaking from traditional thinking and following your passion brings great rewards and true happiness. In this great story, Remy is a rat with the dream of one day becoming a cook. The other rats in his family however just tell him to "be a good rat and eat your garbage". Remy rebels against the opinion of the majority in his pack and soon after, through hard work and an individual way of thinking, he is able to live his dream and become a chef at the best restaurant in Paris. His Family ends up seeing his greatness and his individuality is finally appreciated.

Comments: Excellent introductory sentence that provides an overview of the film before getting down to plot details. "Ratatouille sends the message that breaking from traditional thinking and following your passion brings great rewards and true happiness." And you thought the film was just about a cartoon rat in a kitchen!

Dark Knight

Erik Y — One convincing example that progress is only capable through sacrifice is shown in the movie, *The Dark Knight*. Throughout the film, the heroic vigilante Batman faces his arch-nemesis, the Joker, an anarchist whose sole purpose is to "set fire to the establishment." The idea of a masked vigilante seems to threaten the citizens of Gotham City because Batman acts as though he is above the law. Instead, the people of Gotham turn to District Attorney Harvey Dent, a man so untainted from corrupt business that he is coined the "White Knight." Towards the end of the movie, Joker's ability to manipulate the emotions of others eventually transforms Dent into something different than the public perceives him, a two-faced madman. Upon Dent's death, in order to preserve the image of Dent as someone who can be the driving cause for change, Batman takes the blame for his death by assuming the role as the "Dark Knight." Batman's ability to stand for something deeper than just an image of peace, but rather a man of action and justice makes him a hero, but in the eyes of others he becomes a convicted man on the run. Although Batman loses his heroic image by becoming a convict, this sacrifice preserves the idea of change set forth by Dent in Gotham City.

Comments: Wow. If you thought the previous paragraph on Ratatouille was deep, check this paragraph out. Erik's psychological portrait of Batman gives the crime-fighter a brooding, dialectical edge. Good and evil exist side by side in Chris Nolan's film and Erik does an excellent job of describing the internal conflict Batman experience's before finally assuming the role of the Dark Knight. An existential action hero!

Avatar

Ian W — Another example of the majority's opinion leading society astray is in the film *Avatar*. The James Cameron plot revolves around a group of interstellar miners colonizing a planet to strip it of the rare resource, "unobtanium." Although the mining corporation sees no problems with destroying the primitive natives to obtain the rare resource, the protagonist becomes assimilated in to their culture and gains a sense that the natives are not the savages that the colonists view them as, but are in fact a proud species not too different from ourselves. Had the miners succeeded, a small but noble group would have been annihilated at the hands of the greedy, self-serving majority.

Comments: A lot of my students used *Avatar* as a content example for their SAT essays. Why? Because of all the drama inherent in the screenplay. Although promoted as a whiz-bang 3D adventure film, *Avatar* is really an old-fashioned morality play, as Ian makes clear in his last sentence. "Had the miners succeeded, a small but noble group would have been annihilated at the hands of the greedy, self-serving majority."

Music

In this section, music by the following singers/rappers is employed by student writers in content examples to support various topics:

- Notorious B.I.G
- 2Pac
- Eminem
- Beatles
- Elvis
- Rock 'n Roll
- Stevie Wonder
- Lady Gaga
- George Beauchamp

- Steve Saunders
- Jazz
- Jimi

Biggie

Matthew DLH —The late rapper The Notorious B.I.G, one of the most successful rappers of all time, was no stranger to influence. Born in 1972 in Brooklyn, New York as Christopher Wallace, B.I.G. was caught up in an ever growing drug trade, and was selling crack on the streets at age 17. Eventually, Wallace was sent to jail for 3 years; however, while he was there, Wallace learned to express his emotions through writing. After getting out of prison, B.I.G. started rapping full time and started gaining popularity over a large audience. This way of going against a customary way of life and finding something he could truly excel at lead Biggie Smalls to become one of the most renowned and popular rappers of all time. However, this popularity did not come without misfortune; Biggie was involved in the worst rivalries in the music business. Tragically, this fame ultimately caused him to pay the final price when he was murdered outside of an LA club when he was only 23 years old. In the words of The Notorious B.I.G himself, "You're nobody 'til somebody kills you."

Comments: Talk about great quotes: "You're nobody 'til somebody kills you." -- that takes the cake. This paragraph is a great encapsulation of Biggie's life and times, especially poignant for Readers who might sympathize with the writer, thinking him or her to be African-American. In fact, one of my students, whose complete essay we'll see in the next chapter, wrote about Tupac and got a perfect score (12).

Eminem

Peter J — Another example of this universal truth is shown through the story of Eminem. Throughout his life Marshall Mathers had been discriminated against, growing up in a town where he was the only white kid on the block. Furthermore Eminem aspired to be a famous rapper. Finally after a year of being addicted to cocaine Marshall found the key to his success. Since he couldn't be like all other black rappers, he used a combination of his creativity and anger to create some of the most influential rap lyrics in the history of the concept. In 1995 he released his first album the Slim Shady LP which was a huge hit. When later asked about the key to his success he said that he all he did was kept his head high and believed that he could achieve his goal eventually.

Comments: For purposes of diversity, it's only fair to include a white rapper in the mix. Lots of good subordination and transitions in this paragraph. Notice the variety in sentence structure; aside from the intro, not a single sentence starts off with the subject. Check it out: "Throughout . . Furthermore . . . Finally . . . Since . . . In . . . When". Nice diversity of syntax, nice word flow.

Beatles

Mikk O — Music is a perfect example of society benefiting from goals. If musicians didn't write new songs, there wouldn't be any music. The Beatles truly show how making goals can change the world. With over twenty-five number one hits, with songs like Let it Be and Hey Jude, the song-writing duo of John Lennon and Paul McCartney were unstoppable. This success inspired many young songwriters, therefore bringing new fantastic bands like Led Zeppelin and Queen into the world. To put it simply, without the four Beatle members' goal of changing the world through music, we as a society wouldn't be the same. This success is truly for the record books.

Comments: This paragraph is almost a template for anyone who wants to use music as a pet paragraph. Change Beatles to Elvis or the Rolling Stones or Bruce Springsteen or U2 or whomever and simply reprise their major hits and effect on society.

Elvis

Chris R — Finally the immortal Elvis Presley illustrates how creativity can alter the world around us. Elvis created an entirely original type of music by creatively combining the blues and rhythm into an intriguing new sound that captured the attention of the world. His flamboyant singing and dancing enthralled the new generation who would go on to become the counter-culture rebellion. His creativity would inspire many people who would go on to play in bands like The Beatles, The Rolling Stones, The Eagles, Led Zeppelin, and The Who. If Elvis had not dared to be great, through creativity, the world as we know it would not be the same.

Comments: Chris gets to the heart of Elvis' creative strength when he says Elvis combined "blues and rhythm into an intriguing new sound that captured the attention of the world". Then he puts Elvis into social context by saying he "enthralled the new generation who would go on to become the counter-culture rebellion". Nice sweep.

Rock 'n Roll

Griffin B — The development of Rock and Roll during the 1960's youth movement is prime example of the individual contributing the success of the whole. Bands such as the Who, the Rolling Stones, the Jimi Hendrix Experience and many others developed a unique sound and culture that the world had not yet seen. Through the beautifully orchestrated songs and albums that these individuals wrote on their own, they were able to alter not only revolutionize the music industry, but were also able to create a new outlook on politics and individual morality as well. Although looked down on disgustedly by many, new techniques of distortion and nonlinear rhythms transported the listener to new spiritual heights. Pete Townshend and Jimi Hendrix were particularly important in the revolution of rock and roll through their uncanny stage behavior and virtuoso playing skills. If these individuals had not stepped outside the social norms of the music industry culture would have not progressed nearly to as great of an extent as it has which emphasizes the fact that individuals can have a substantial impact on the whole of society.

Comments: Rather than focusing on individuals, Griffin takes a broad-brush approach and paints a vivid picture of Rock 'n Roll's impact on American culture.

Stevie Wonder

Eric K — Finally, a last example of creativity playing an important role is shown through the musical talent of Stevie Wonder. Not only has Stevie Wonder learned to live with and conquer his blindness, he has done it in a way that has blessed and bestowed his audience with the gift of hope. Stevie Wonder is an American singer-songwriter, multi-instrumentalist, record producer and activist. Rather than burdening himself with his disability, he uses it to his advantage in the most creative way possible- music. His creativity is displayed through the way he plays, because rather than reading notes off a page, something he is physically unable to do, he feels what he performs and more effectively connects to his audience.

Comments: Eric plays the disadvantaged card here saying "Rather than burdening himself with his disability, he uses it to his advantage . . .". Tugs on the heartstrings of the Readers.

Lady Gaga

Gabby B— Another example of avant-garde expression is Lady Gaga, a rising pop sensation throughout the world who has changed the conventional definition of pop music. Lady Gaga was the first female artist to cover her body in tattoos as well as cover her face in masks, bejeweled sunglasses, or with exotic makeup designs. She also revolutionized pop-culture with her wild and imaginative hairstyles and outfits. Lady Gaga is the first performer to make a hat out of her own hair, as well as the only celebrity to ever sport heelless platform shoes. While some may see her as obnoxious and outlandish, no one can deny that she has left a lasting impact on pop culture that will forever change the way it is perceived by future generations. It takes an unconventional mind to create a new genre of music and a new standard of what is socially acceptable among celebrities.

Comments: Gabby pulled out all the stops to present Lady Gaga as both a cultural icon and a musical force of nature. Excellent phrasing ("avant-garde expression") and wonderful detail concerning her impact on not just music but also fashion and design.

George Beauchamp

Josh L — In 1931, George Beauchamp developed a new form of sound that brought the guitar into the twentieth century. This new idea was called the electric guitar. This musical instrument was the beginning of many complex genres of music such as Rock 'n Roll, Jazz, and many other classes of song. Beauchamp gave the guitar limitless volume and sharp tone. In addition, the electric guitar catalyzed an era of other electric instruments such as the synthesizer, the keyboard and various other advanced plug-ins. This shows how a new perspective of an instrument can transform the entire music industry.

Comments: This back-story paragraph on the technical beginnings of Rock 'n Roll is oustanding. Nice phrasing: "the electric guitar catalyzed an era of other electric instruments . . ."

Steve Saunders

Mallory L — We see creativity lead into progress in the world of pop culture. In the creation of the bass line for Michael Jackson's hit "Billie Jean," Steve Saunders, one of the top engineers for the Yamaha X80 keyboard, was asked to create a sound that sounded like "someone was strumming the cables of the Golden Gate bridge." He and another top engineer for the Yamaha X80, Sean Vanduren, successfully created this sound in 1983, after toying with their keyboards for hours on end. After its creation, "Bille Jean" rocked the charts and the same exact sound has been used in hundreds, if not thousands, of other songs since the idea was first implemented on the Yamaha keyboard in 1983. Hence, one sound lead to a plethora of new ones and new technology, further proving that progress follows creativity.

Comments: Like Josh's paragraph on George Beauchamp, Mallory goes straight to the technical heart of pop music in this pet paragraph, giving the reader remarkable insight into the technical aspects of music production.

Jazz

Manuel H — Jazz music, like any form of music, is a form of creativity which creates beauty with the power of bringing people together and bringing joy to those who have none. Jazz is a creative form of language or more precisely, a conversation. It is an improvised conversation between a trumpeter, a precisionist, a jazz pianist, and a saxophonist. It is an art not based so much on repetition, practice, and perfection, but pure creativity. Jazz, though a uniquely American art form, spread to Europe and merged with other art forms in Latin America. Jazz is the coming together of not just white American culture Black American cultures, but all peoples. The conflict Jazz faced in its heyday in the 30s was to entertain a distressed population. But the dancing and the smiles continued in the 30s as it had done in the 30s, where jazz music played. Creativity in music had the power not only to bond but to keep people going.

Comments: This paragraph brings dramatic insight to jazz, which is a "creative form of language or more precisely, a conversation." Great cultural and artistic sweep.

Jimi

Matt B — Finally, creativity as a means to progress can be seen in the guitar legend, Jimi Hendrix. No guitarist has ever revolutionized rock music more than Hendrix. With his use of new amplifier feedback techniques, which were previously deemed undesirable, and his fusion of blues, R&B, soul, funk, and jazz, Jimi Hendrix forever changed the face of Rock'n'Roll. His original music and lyrics brought him much success and also influenced other musicians such as Stevie Ray Vaughn, Jimmy Page, and Eric Clapton. Hendrix will forever be known for his revolutionary take on music and how he popularized the distinct sound of Rock.

Comments: Jimi! Enough said.

Sports

In this section, the following athletes and coaches are introduced by student writers in content examples to support various topics:

- Emmitt Smith
- Standford/Cal football
- Jackie Robinson
- Coach Herman Boone
- Manager Mike Scioscia

Emmit Smith

Kelly M — Emmitt Smith, the National Football League's all-time leading rusher, attributes his success on and off the field solely to the goals that he set for himself as a child. In his Hall Of Fame Inductee speech, he acclaimed goal setting over and over again, and attributed his phenomenal success purely to writing down his goals for the rest of his life at a young age. Smith claims that as a young boy he told his dad that one day he wanted to play in the National Football League on the Dallas Cowboys. Then in high school he wrote down his goals in life – One of which was to become the all-time leading rusher, win a championship, and be named MVP. Not only did he reach his goals, but he surpassed them with flying colors, winning three championships, having two MVP awards to his name, and obliterating the rushing record previously held by Walter Peyton – Emmitt's idol when growing up. He was also drafted by his 'dream team', the Dallas cowboys, and stayed in their organization throughout his career.

Comments: Kelly follows the life of Emmit Smith from childhood to adolescence to adulthood, noting his remarkable achievements along the way.

Stanford/Cal Football

Eric K—Another example of human success depending on people's creativity is the rivalry game between Stanford and Cal in 1980. The bitter rivalry did not disappoint in making a dramatic game with the teams exchanging the lead multiple times. In the dying seconds, it seemed that Cal would be the sure victor, but Stanford made a crucial field goal to take the lead 20-19. With only four seconds left on the clock, Cal's special team's coach Paul Thomson pulled aside his players and drew up what seemed to be an impossible play. When they received the kick-off, the players made a run for the end zone. With the clock running out, the defense swarmed the ball carrier, but at the last second he threw a lateral pass to another player. Cal threw five laterals in the single play to march their way into the end-zone and history. Thomson's incredible imagination helped himself and the team create one of the most memorable game ending plays ever.

Comments: Excellent description of the last-second highly-controversial play that allowed Cal to beat Stanford in the 1982 Big Game. Lotta drama, folks.

Jackie Robinson

Carl K — Furthermore back in 1940, African Americans were not allowed to play in the Major Leagues simply because of the color of their skin. However, in late 1940, a courageous young African American man by the name of Jackie Robinson decided that his love for the game would overpower the hatred and racism of the time. An unbelievably athletic shortstop with a sharp knack for the game, Robinson, despite his race, could not be turned down by Los Angeles Dodgers GM Robert Johns. Although Jackie Robinson had become the first African American to make it to the Major Leagues, his troubles had just begun. For Jackie Robinson, the days that followed consisted of constant ridicule filled with racial slurs. Furthermore, Jackie's mailbox would be filled day after day with death threats to both him and his family. Yet Robinson swallowed his pride and chose to silence his critics by posting up MVP callibur numbers within his first year in the majors, which led to his winning of the National League Rookie of the Year Award. In the proceeding years, because of Robinson's trailblazing for the rest of the African American community, baseball's African American population grew exponentially. Robinson used his creativity to challenge authority by sacrificing his personal pride and health in order to cause change in something he believed in.

Comments: This is an extremely-detailed account of how one African American overcame racism and long odds to challenge baseball's color line is a super example of how to utilize sports figures (black or white, for that matter) in an SAT essay. Excellent transitions and subordination throughout. Also some nice phrasing, as in "baseball's African American population grew exponentially".

Coach Herman Boone

Jessica W — Finally, pop culture demonstrates society's new acceptance toward African Americans in the film, *Remember the Titans*. In this popular movie, a racial segregated community in Louisiana must learn to forget their traditional discrimination and accept a more open and diverse lifestyle, thanks to the arrival of an inspiring African American football coach. Because the Caucasian and African American athletes had a history of picking fights on each other, the new football coach, Herman Boone, believes he can change these corrupted teenage minds. With a summer long disciplinary camp, Coach Boone accomplishes his mission for the team; yet the worst is still to come. The second after the now colorblind team sets foot hand in hand, the remainder of the town is in outraged pandemonium. Eventually, Coach Boone and his team champion for their new mind set and transform the town into the least segregated town in the United States. Obviously, with a little determination and a new clean mind set, society can progress from violence to peace.

Comments: Excellent recap of the film. I put this paragraph under Sports since it's really about Coach Herman Boone who "accomplishes his mission for the team; yet the worst is still to come'" Nice dramatic tension after the semicolon.

Manager Mike Scioscia

Matt B — Also, since the 1990s Major League Baseball has been plagued by the effects of a steroid epidemic, yet in the middle of the steroid era, Mike Scioscia was able to use a creative uncommon strategy to lead his team to its first World Series victory in franchise history. Scioscia's 2002 Angels employed a strategy known as "small ball" in which the team tries to place runners on base and move them over in a methodical way, typically with bunts and stolen bases. This philosophy centers around a good pitching staff, consistent and fast hitters, and a lack of power in the lineup. While this strategy was not new, it was uncommon in the steroid era where home runs were the preferred method of scoring. Despite hitting the least home runs in the league, the Angels won the World Series as a result of their league leading ERA, Stolen Bases, and Sacrifice Bunts. Through the use of a creative and unconventional strategy, Angels manager Mike Scioscia led his ballclub to unexpected success.

Comments: Great description of "small ball" and the ingenous philosophy behind it. Way to go, Matt!

Technology

In this section, the following topics are covered by student writers in content examples to support various topics:

- Microsoft
- Apple
- Facebook
- Post-Its
- Wright Brothers
- Gutenberg
- BP Oil Spill
- Columbia Space Shuttle
- Chernobyl
- Titanic

Microsoft

Erin C — There are many individuals who are admired and have become famous through the use of others' work, and, disregarding moral qualms, this is definitely the way to go. Bill Gates, for example, could be titled an "idea stealer", but instead, everyone appreciates his brilliance and significance. If you dug deep into the history of computer software, you'd realize that Apple Computers originally developed the software that allows people to navigate computers efficiently and easily. However, Bill Gates and the Microsoft Company used this information and technology to make extravagant profits. If it wasn't for Microsoft's "stealing" of this idea, computers and that technology may not have been so widely distributed among the common man as they are today. There is no doubt that Bill Gates achieved something significant by using the ideas put forward by Apple.

Comments: I love this content example from Erin since it SO demythologizes Bill Gates and pulls no punches in revealing the devious means by which Microsoft pilfered the design of Apple's user-friendly interface.

Apple

Krissy L — Another compelling illustration of the importance of creativity in our world today is the success of the technological company Apple, Inc. and its founder, Steve Jobs. Jobs founded the company in the late 1970s, and it has transformed over the last forty years into one of the largest and most successful electronics and technology production companies in the world. Apple, Inc. has created products such as the iPhone, iPod, and Macbook which serve a purpose in education, entertainment, and business. These products are unlike any other in the world of modern technology because they have features beyond that of past computers. Apple's products are so advanced that other brands can barely compete with their exceptional ideas. Without the creative minds fueling Apple's production, the company might have failed decades ago and the technology of the present world would be drastically different.

Comments: Nice history and evolution of Apple computer with props to Steve Jobs, much more a pioner and visionary than Bill Gates. Notice how Krissy loads the paragraph with significant detail, including items from the product line. Inclusion of concrete detail (iPhone, iPod, and Macbook) is the mark of a good writer.

Facebook

Amanda C — Lastly, creativity's ability to revolutionize the world is seen in the internet phenomenon, Facebook. Created only six years ago by the college student Mark Zuckerburg, the social networking site was once a small idea, overshadowed by the powerful MySpace. Now, Facebook has transcended MySpace in order to become a worldwide internet site with millions of users. Everyday, more and more people are joining Facebook and Facebook vernacular has become a part of everyday conversations. Zuckerberg even said, "How on earth did we stalk our exes, remember our co-workers birthdays, or bug our friends before Facebook?" Facebook has truly changed the world through its creative content and ideas.

Comments: Superb paragraph on the evolution of Facebook. Nice vocab -- "vernacular" -- and terrific quote from Zuckerberg.

Post-Its

Ryan A — Creativity is also beneficial in less destructive and dire situations, such as in the workplace. In the 1970s, computers were still quite a few years from being used by businesses. Therefore, it made organization and time management difficult. But, when 3M employee Art Fry discovered his coworker Spencer Silvers failed attempt at a glue product, he decided to use the weak glue to stick self-notes to the wall of his cubicle. He decided to call these notes Post-Its, and his new invention spread rapidly across the country. Suddenly, people no longer had to sort through files or stacks of papers to remind themselves when their meetings were: Everything they needed to know was on a little yellow paper right in front of them. Thanks to Fry's creative thinking, storing information in your office suddenly had a far more practical solution.

Comments: Well, Romy and Michelle notwithstanding, Ryan has written the definitive short history of Post-Its here. Extremely fluid writing style with excellent transitions (therefore, suddenly), great sentence variety and concrete detail.

Wright Brothers

Krissy L — One example of a new idea that drastically changed our lives today was the invention of the fixed-wing aircraft by the Wright brothers, Orville and Wilbur. In the early 1900s, the Wright brothers worked endlessly to create a new form of transportation that would be more convenient than any land or water based transportation. Although the brothers failed many times to produce a working aircraft that would allow humans to fly, on December 17, 1903 they successfully invented and built the world's first airplane. Without air travel, it would take hours or days to travel throughout the world resulting in a less unified and educated globe. The Wright brothers' unique ideas to allow humans to fly began a new age of transportation that made almost anything possible.

Comments: Nothing fancy here, just a cleanly-written, straight-forward history of the brothers Wright.

Gutenberg

Logan E — Progress in literature coincides with the progress of education. In 1456, the most imortant invention was created, the Gutenburg printing press. This invention was sparked by a new idea that with more printings more people could read the Bible. Now that more books, pamphlets, music were being printed new ideas and concepts were traveling around the European continent. Books were no longer written in Latin but in the vernacular for everyday people to read. The new idea of mass producing changed the progress of society to a faster moving one where information and communication could prosper.

Comments: Nice, crisp writing about the guy who made this book possible by inventing the printing press. Thanks, Gutenberg.

BP Oil Spill

Julia W — Our world's environmental crisis is at the worst that the human race has ever witnessed it before, especially with the recent BP oil spill, named the worst in the history of America. Creativity is required for new solutions to help assuage the damage of this spill; older solutions that may have once been successful are deemed useless in their trials to contain this spill. Many different methods have been utilized, attempting to plug the leaks in the fallen oil rig. Recent attempts such as constructing a giant dome, spraying the waters with chemical dispersants, and plugging up the leaks with trash such as tires and rope have all failed. Needed more than ever today are novel notions and creative solutions that are more likely to solve this leak.

Comments: Excellent vocab: "help assuage the damage of this spill". Excellent parellel structure: "Recent attempts such as constructing a giant dome, spraying the waters with chemical dispersants, and plugging up the leaks with trash such as tires and rope have all failed." Excellent job.

Columbia Space Shuttle

Angelika K— One instance which illustrates that "no progress is possible without sacrifice" is the unfortunate fate of the Columbia space shuttle. Although the shuttle was equipped with the finest technology and the most experienced crew available, nobody could prevent the malfunction which destroyed the shuttle and its crew. This disaster resulted in great financial damage to NASA. Although this experience was unpleasant, NASA technicians conducted tests to find out what had gone wrong with Columbia so that they could improve future missions. This research resulted in the recent successful launch of the Arizona space shuttle. Thus, although the Columbia accident was a tragedy, it also helped NASA make progress.

Comments: Good transitions, excellent writing and a good recounting of the disaster while staying close to the topic at hand. The reference to the "Arizona" space shuttle, which doesn't exist, is OK since the readers are instructed not to take points off for technical inaccuracies.

Jeremy P — The first example of the notion that we learn from our mistakes occurred in 2003 when disaster struck the Space Shuttle Columbia. During takeoff a piece of foam, weighing almost two pounds, detached from the fuel tank of the shuttle and hit the left wing creating a large hole. Nothing was thought of the incident as the flight was going according to plan. It was not until the shuttle was returning to Earth that a problem was evident. The hole created in the heat protective shield of the wing allowed the wing to become exceedingly hot. So hot in fact that all the sensors in the left wing lost contact with NASA as well as the astronauts themselves. Soon afterwards the crew lost contact with ground control completely. The crew was now flying over 200,000 feet above the earth at a speed of Mach 18, without any control of the plane. The heat eventually melted the shuttle in the air and all the astronauts were killed. This loss lead NASA to conduct numerous tests and design the Shuttle over again so as to avoid such a tragedy. If this had not happened the new designs and technology used on the next shuttle would not have been thought of and put into place.

Comments: Super descriptions and excellent writing. For example: "During takeoff a piece of foam, weighing almost two pounds, detached from the fuel tank of the shuttle and hit the left wing creating a large hole." As far as attention to detail goes, it doesn't get any better than that.

Chernobyl

Rob G — Another depiction of the notion that progress is met with sacrifices can be seen in the major nuclear meltdown at Chernobyl. During the early 1980's technological advancements set nuclear power on the fast track to success. Yet, for all the scientific progress made in the field to keep nuclear power safe, in 1986 the power plant in Chernobyl, Ukraine exploded. A series of operator actions, including the disabling of automatic shutdown mechanisms led to the release of deadly fission products into the atmosphere. This left hundreds dead and caused severe fallout all over the city. Even though we made lengthy progress in nuclear power we were met with sacrifices: thirty people killed and thousands contaminated with radiation.

Comments: Excellent writing. Nice detail with descriptions such as ". . . the disabling of automatic shutdown mechanisms led to the release of deadly fission products into the atmosphere. Also, good transitions such as "Yet, for all the scientific progress made in the field . . ." Excellent support for the topic.

Kent H — One illustration of the credo that progress can only be made through new ideas can be seen in the Manhattan Project, a scientific movement to create the atomic bomb. Led by J. Robert Oppenheimer and Albert Einstein, a group of scientists worked long and hard to come up with new mathematical equations and ideas to apply to the creation of the bomb. With their newly constructed theories, the scientists were able to make the first atomic bomb. Such progress in the field of science had many practical implications and was only possible because of the revolutionary thoughts of the scientists involved.

Comments: Exceptionally clear and concise writing with excellent subordination. Notice Kent's use of an appositive (in italics) in the first sentence: "One illustration of the credo that progress can only be made through new ideas can be seen in the Manhattan Project, *a scientific movement to create the atomic bomb.*"

Titanic

Conor W — A clear illustration of the theme that appearances can be deceiving occurs in the history of the Titanic. The Titanic was a ship presumed to be unsinkable due to different chambers that would allow the hull to be breached without sinking. However, the appearance of the Titanic fooled hundreds of passengers, for when it hit an iceberg, the chambers filled and dragged the ship down slowly. If people had been initially more skeptical of the massive ship, there is a distinct possibility that the horrendous accident would never have occurred. This clearly shows how disaster and loss of life can occur when someone accepts an initial appearance without further investigation.

Comments: Excellent detail concerning the physical structure of the ship: "different chambers that would allow the hull to be breached". Good transitions and strong narrative support for the theme that appearances can be deceptive.

Art

In this section, the following topics are covered by student writers in content examples to support various topics:

- Andy Warhol
- Propaganda
- Evolution of Art
- Picasso

Andy Warhol

Mellissa M — Previous to the nineteen sixties, art was considered to reflect emotion, knowledge and beauty. Andy Warhol, however, chose to redefine art by "thinking outside the box". Andy Warhol, an enigmatic artist during the sixties and seventies influenced artists around the world to create a new style of art, Pop Art. Warhol advanced the idea of art by creating a new artistic twist by using vibrant colors, and familiar objects and celebrities as his subject. His portrait of Marilyn Monroe is praised by fans everywhere. If Andy Warhol had conformed to the typical style of art, and didn't create Pop Art, then he would not have progressed art to the level it is at now.

Comments: This paragraph is characterized by excellent vocab — "enigmatic artist", "vibrant colors"— and a sophisticated view of Andy Warhol as the progenitor of Pop Art. The theme of creativity is emphasized through wonderful and sophisticated writing.

Propaganda

Logan E— The role of art is to inspire and to be creative, it's also the backbone of society. It is responsible for creating progress of a whole group or nation by explaining and inspiring with new ideas. Propaganda, is possibly the best persuasive form of art to contain a group from outside ideas. Propaganda was used in the world wars to bring an idea to the nation's people that the other countries were evil. This idea led to the total war effort and with ensuing progress won the war. This tactic is still used today, and what is modern day propaganda but advertising. Advertising is just new ideas to sell and persuade you to buy a certain product. A company's yearly progressive income relies on how well they can sell you their ideas.

Comments: Logan turns the idea of Art upside down in the pet paragraph, arguing that art, meant to inspire new ideas, can also be co-opted by the establishment and turned into propaganda for war or advertising for commerce.

Evolution of Art

Cameron B— No region better displays this than art. Art chiefly evolves through the synthesis of old and new ideas-impressionism — but occasionally artists leave the old behind altogether for the strange and new — cubism. Art is a mirror for the era in which it is painted. As change comes to an era, art too must change in order to properly evoke the feelings of the period. When the Plague forced people to reconsider their lifestyle, art reflected and responded to this change in outlook. Art began to focus more on the secular, and new artistic tools were invented — such as perspective — to further the feelings of non-religious paintings. Later, as society began to fragment, it was reflected in the ever-more fragmented cubism and counter-culture of Dadaism. Art represents and mirrors progress like no other, and artists are particularly apt at fusing ideas to create something original, progress at its purist.

Comments: Cameron gets to the heart of the matter with this nicely symetrical comment: "Art is a mirror for the era in which it is painted. As change comes to an era, art too must change in order to properly evoke the feelings of the period." A lesser writer might have simply left it at that. But Cameron supplies excellent concrete detail to back this thesis up, commenting on the Plague, use of perspective, cubism and Dadaism. Great sweep.

Picasso

Katie J — Famous artist Pablo Picasso also highlights the importance of creativity. In the beginning of his painting career, Picasso did unoriginal work. Though it was apparent he was extraordinarily talented, the pieces lacked creativity and originality. Later, he started to experiment with his art, resulting in the outcome of his most famous pieces. Picasso's incomparable creativity not only resulted in beautiful artwork but he created an entirely new style of abstract artistry. His inspiring work forever changed the world of art and made our culture more rich and multifaceted.

Comments: What better way to conclude this section on art than with a paragraph on the master, Picasso. The only thing I'd suggest here to improve the paragraph would be more detail about some of the famous pieces mentioned. In other words, a passing mention of works like *Guernica* or the *Portrait of Dora Mar* would work to round out the description and lend a greater air of authority.

History

In this section, the following historical topics are covered by student writers in content examples to support various topics:

* Civil Rights
* Ghandi
* Barak Obama
* Women's Rights
* FDR
* 9/11
* Revolutionary War
* World War II
* World War I
* Industrial Revolution
* Transcendentalism
* Scientific Revolution
* Agricultural Revolution
* Civil War
* Columbus
* Renaissance
* Harriet Tubman
* South Africa
* Nelson Mandela
* Somali Pirates
* SALT I and II

≡

- Hitler
- Japanese Internment Camps
- John Adams

Civil Rights

Brett W — The theme of the failure of our best-prepared plans is also illustrated throughout history. After The Civil War, during the reconstruction period, the south was devastated. The southern economy was in ruin, and the major labor force in the south was now free. Slavery was banished in the United States by the thirteenth Amendment in 1863. The congressional plan for reconstruction called for the betterment of blacks in society. The fifteenth amendment permitted blacks to vote in government elections. Congress eventually established the Freedmen's Bureau to regulate the treatment of blacks in southern society, ensuring them equal rights. Unfortunately, Southern whites implemented laws restricting blacks' rights to vote through laws such as the Jim Crow laws and the Grandfather clause. Blacks were also harassed at the voting booths when trying to cast their votes. The congressional plan for integrating blacks into society was foiled by racist southerners and ex-confederates.

Comments: Wonderful detail and polished, straightforward writing. Notice how smoothly Brett presents his facts and then turns the tables with a transition beginning with "Unfortunately, Southern whites implemented laws restricting blacks' rights to vote through laws such as the Jim Crow laws and the Grandfather clause." An excellent example showing how the best laid plans sometimes go wrong.

Colleen M — One compelling illustration that appearances can cloud reality is shown in the Supreme Court case of 1843, Plessy verses Ferguson. This case stated that separate facilities for blacks and whites were constitutional as long as they were created equal. On first appearance this "separate but equal" doctrine seemed fair. However, after further examination, people began to see that this inherent equality did not exist. The separate facilities for African Americans deteriorated and were not nearly as "equal" as some presumed. This case created the illusion that African Americans and whites were equal however in reality true equality was not created.

Comments: This final example of a Civil Rights paragraph is stunning in its straightforward simplicity. Colleen manages to cover the legal grounds for the "separate but equal" doctrine with clarity and style. I paticularly like the transition "However, after further examination, . . ." Brilliant writing.

Ghandi

Mark C — Today and throughout history, oppressed people set and pursue goals of freedom. In the 19th century during European imperialism, the British took control of India. As a British colony, India began to resent foreign domination. During the Indian Independence Movement in the 1920's, Mahatma Gandhi, India's political and spiritual leader set and pursued goals to achieve self-rule. His innovative idea of civil disobedience used non-violence to bring about needed change. Gandhi said, "Nonviolence and truth are inseparable." Calling on Indians to boycott British goods especially British cloth, Handy urged Indians to weave their own cloth. In fact the peaceful spinning wheel was used as a symbol of Indian resistance to British rule. In addition to boycotts, Gandhi asked Indians to strike and demonstrate to achieve their objectives. The Indians could only buy salt from the British government so Gandhi and his followers walked 240 miles to the seacoast to make their own salt during the Salt March of 1930. British police officers with steel clubs attacked the peaceful demonstrators, but Gandhi and his followers held fast to their goals and refused to defend themselves and their attackers. The Indians' peaceful resistance gained worldwide support for Gandhi's movement. By pursuing their goals, Indians eventually gained independence.

Comments: Extremely detailed and beautifully written paragraph on Ghandi. Excellent description of the famous Salt March. This paragraph, like many others to follow in this section, shows the value in taking AP Euro your junior year. Not only does it contribute to stunningly detailed SAT essays, it also gives you a perspective on the world most American high school students are sorely lacking.

Barak Obama

Dani V — Similar to the caste system in Ancient India, our modern world is still suffering the effects of a class system. Generally you are born into your family's wealth and class, making it hard to escape from this vicious circle. However, Barack Obama, a modern day hero had his goals and priorities set from a young age. Living in a poor African American family he had a hard child-hood, but had unwavering motivation to thrive. He wanted to live the American dream, break away from his family's path and succeed. He is not a hero because the color of his skin, but because he has paved a road for under privileged minorities across the world and has maintained his morals and integrity while still being a successful president. He acted as the perfect counter attack to the Bush administrations' faulty rule from 2000-2008. He has made a mark in history that will never be forgotten and will forever change the normalities of our culture and government.

Comments: Interesting analogy -- "Similar to the caste system in Ancient India, our modern world . . . " Nice vocab: "vicious circle". Good writing.

≡

Women's Rights

Nikki K — One compelling illustration that some failure always accompanies progress is demonstrated in the Women's Rights movement. Around the 1930s women started to question their role in society. Why were women not allowed a say in the government? Why couldn't men and women possess the same rights? During a protest in front of the White House, women were arrested and sent to a special prison. In order to become noticed, the National Women's Rights association in a literal sense sacrificed those who were arrested and replaced them with more women. This process repeated itself until, Alice Paul, a Women's Rights leader, protested in front of the White House herself. She joined her comrades in the prison, where they were abused and mistreated. Finally once their mistreatment was exposed to the public, the President of the United States set them free and granted their wishes of equality and rights. Their sacrifices were not in vain as the women were able to accomplish their goal and change the country forever.

Comments: Nikki makes terrific use of rhetorical questions to make her case. For example: "Why were women not allowed a say in the government?" and "Why couldn't men and women possess the same rights?". Terrific job.

FDR

Sara H — Franklin Delano Roosevelt was yet another historical figure that used his optimistic spirit to motivate the nation when, unexpectedly, things shifted in the wrong direction. The abrupt crash of the Stock Market in 1929, which ignited the turbulent and trying Great Depression, sent the United States into a financial downfall. If not for FDR's implementation of the New Deal, an ambitious plan striving for economic recovery, the Great Depression would have augmented the already severe impact it had on American citizens. By staying hopeful, perseverant, and positive during the tumultuous years of the Great Depression, FDR was able to succeed in his political endeavors and sustain a national unity despite the difficulties of that time period.

Comments: Excellent vocab, sentence variety and parallel structure as evidenced in the last sentence: "By staying hopeful, perseverant, and positive during the tumultuous years of the Great Depression, FDR was able to succeed in his political endeavors and sustain a national unity despite the difficulties of that time period. " Wow!

911

Beth G — A final illustration that heroes are an important aspect of current society occurred on September 11, 2001. A day that will go down in history: two planes crashed into New York City's Twin Towers and killed thousands, affecting millions. A day that called upon the people known as New York's finest: the police and fire department, paramedics, doctors, and even civilians. Everyone, despite their differences, came together for one cause: to help those in need stuck in the towers. People gave out food and water to the hundreds of volunteers that came to Ground Zero in order to search for the bodies of loved ones. That day, everyone, with and without a badge, became a hero, and without their efforts the effect could have been much worse.

Comments: Interesting writing style. Beth uses parallel structure and repetion ("A day that . . .") to make a strong emotional point. Very effective.

Revolutionary War

Kent H — Another illustration of the sacrifice involved in progress can be seen in the historical Revolutionary War. 1775 and 1776 proved to be two important years for the thirteen colonies that would soon be known collectively as the United States of America. Troops led by generals such as George Washington and William Prescott fought daringly against the British Army along the Eastern Coast of North America. At the Battle of Bunker Hill, General Prescott said to his troops, "Don't shoot until you see the whites of their eyes." This daring command exemplifies the notion that progress, or freedom in this case, could only be achieved through the sacrifice of human lives in close-range warfare.

Comments: This is a wonderful, novelistic description of the Revolutionary War. Excellent (and real) historical quote from General Prescott. Also notice Kent's conclusion, which is picture perfect: "This daring command exemplifies the notion that progress, or freedom in this case, could only be achieved through the sacrifice of human lives in close-range warfare."

World War II

Mark P — The theme that no progress is possible without sacrifice is also seen in the Allied operations in the Second World War. In preparation for the eventual conquest of the European continent, the Allied commanders had decided to eliminate the Axis powers' exterior defences in North Africa, Sicily, and Asia. Once the strategy for Operation Overlord was completed the amassing of Allied forces in England began. On June 6, 1944 after two days of delays, the Allied forces landed on the beaches of Normandy, France and assaulted the Germans' Fortress Europe. During the course of the day the American and British forces underwent heavy casualties on the Omaha, Utah, and Juneau beaches. However, after enormous sacrifice the Allied forces were victorious.

Comments: This is a brilliant, colorful and detailed encapsulation of the Normandy invasion. Tremendous detail. The sentence structure is outstanding: "In preparation for the eventual conquest of the European continent, the Allied commanders had decided to eliminate the Axis powers' exterior defences in North Africa, Sicily, and Asia." Terrific job.

Armeen K —One compelling illustration that appearances are deceptive occurs in the Battle of Iwo Jima between the US Marines and the Imperial Army of Japan. The Marines arrived at Iwo Jima with 70,000 men while the Japanese only had 22,000. Early reconnaissance of the island showed little defense and activity on the island, creating the belief that the island was not well defended. However, this was because the 20,000 Japanese soldiers had dug massive expanses of tunnels throughout the island. The Americans were tricked yet again when they intially tried to bomb the island. Since no Japanese guns fired at planes or ships, the Americans thought that they had silenced their defenses, but this was obviously not the case when the Americans invaded the island. Japanese defenses unleashed mass barrages of fire on to the venerable Americans. After two months of ruthless fighting the Americans had killed 21,800 of the Japanese embedded in the island and lost over 7,000 and had 19,000 wounded. When interviewed by a reporter after the war, Marine Corps Major Stephen Callgary stated, "For every inch of land above the island, the Japanese had dug 10 inches under." This example of appearances and reality cost two nations over 28,000 men.

Comments: Although perhaps too crowded with numeric detail, this paragraph nonetheless provides insight into the strategic moves made by the Japanese during World War II and underscores the deceptive nature of appearances.

World War I

Jesse D — Examples of plans gone awry can also be seen through history. At the beginning of WWI, the German army developed a plan that they thought to be smart, quick and effective. The Schlieffen plan, which was formulated by German General Alfred Von Schlieffen, proposed knocking out France first with a lightening attack through neutral Belgium before turning on Russia. The plan, which seemed foolproof, failed as the Germans faced a surprise when the Belgians defended their homeland. This slowed the Germans down and lead to their loss against the French--and the eventual loss of the war.

Comments: This paragraph shows great attention to detail and nice sentence structure: "The Schlieffen plan, which was formulated by German general Alfred Von Schlieffen, proposed knocking out France first with a lightening attack through neutral Belgium before turning on Russia."

Industrial Revolution

Jessica W — For example, the innovative works of the Industrial Revolution forever changed human existence by pushing technology to the limit. In the 19th century, millions of slaves injured themselves thanks to the vigorous work of handpicking cotton. Fortunately, a famous and brilliant inventor, Eli Whitney, finally created a ground-breaking solution, known as the cotton gin. Furthermore, Eli Whitney needed to think outside of his time's orthodox mind set in order to free millions from the detrimental labor to thrive in more desirable occupations. Several years later, one of the most virtuoso and influential geniuses, Nicholas Ford, created one of society's most profitable and convenient ways of transportation, known as the automobile. Before Ford's invention, carriages and trains were the most popular forms of transportation and a four-wheel personal vehicle was unimaginable. However, with the affordable Model T vehicle, the public could easily commute to work and travel to farther destinations. Revolutionary inventors, like Eli Whitney and Nicholas Ford, have progressed society through their imaginations.

Comments: Check out the transitions and subordinate phrases Jessica provides for every sentence in this perfect description of the Industrial Revolution. I'm gonna list them; see if you can follow along: For example . . . In the 19th century . . . Fortunately . . . Furthermore . . . Several years later . . . Before Ford's invention . . . However. Transitions and subordination: marks of a great writer.

Transcendentalism

Grace M — The philosophy of transcendentalism, as illustrated by the works of Ralph Waldo Emerson, urge men to think freely in order to reach their higher potentials. Emerson states that "whoso must be a man must be a nonconformist" and that "men of tradition are blind herds, swarms" in his essay "Self-Reliance." Thus, Emerson believes that social traditions have a way of trapping men into the perfunctory actions of living without fully utilizing their intellects. When men follow tradition, they fail to think for themselves or follow their own divine intuitions. If a man wants to attain his fullest potentials, he must not blindly conform to social expectations, but become an independent thinker. Such a thinker can utilize his soul, which channels the force of the universe and divinity, to transcend above his earthly limits and imbibe in the absolute truth and perfection of God. Emerson's philosophy stresses the overthrow of traditional thinking. Men who are not afraid of searching for new ideas are the ones who will receive inspiration and enlightenment. With his own progressive philosophy, Emerson revolutionized the American way of thinking, which emphasized individualism and self-trust. Applying his own principles to life, Emerson shows that originality and creativity of mind can truly change the intellectual landscape of an entire nation.

Comments: Grace is back with another philosophical take on the SAT essay. Here she deftly encapsulates the drawbacks of traditional thinking: "Thus, Emerson believes that social traditions have a way of trapping men into the perfunctory actions of living without fully utilizing their intellects." Obviously, Grace does not fall into this trap, utilizing her own to the fullest.

Scientific Revolution

Tasia R — Another revolution occurred in the seventeenth century, with its roots based entirely in the creation of new ideas. This was the Scientific Revolution, and its basis was entirely in the intellectuals and scientists that dared to challenge old, traditional ideas. For example, in 1543, the Copernican hypothesis was published. Copernicus stated three appalling new ideas; firstly, stars only appear to move and they are actually still, secondly, it suggested that the universe was far larger than initially believed, and lastly, it destroyed ideas of earth being special or heavenly by representing it as just another planet. New ideas such as these thoroughly progressed the way people thought, and think today.

Comments: What I love about this description is the itemization of Copernicus' ideas. Most kids mention the heliocentric part of Copernicus' theories and have done with it. Tasia goes the whole nine yards, listing her three new ideas with scientific attention to detail.

Agricultural Revolution

Jason B — One example of using creativity to surmount a difficult task was the Agricultural Revolution. In the seventeenth century, both England and the Netherlands faced a serious dilemma. The two countries experienced a rapidly increasing population while the availability of arable land diminished. In order to supply food to a growing population, the governments of both countries turned to brilliant innovators such as Jethro Tull. Tull used his creativity to devise more efficient methods of farming that would be practiced in Europe centuries into the future. As the British author, D. H. Lawrence, noted, "the ideas of one generation become the instincts of the next." The new ideas of one man became the basis of farming for years to come.

Comments: Once again, AP Euro rules the day. But Jason isn't content with simply stating interesting historical facts. He performs some smooth literary moves at the end of his paragraph, using a quote from the master (D. H. Lawrence) to highlight his perspective on the generational impact of agriculture evolution.

Civil War

Ross K — In the Civil War, General Robert E. Lee of the United States of the Confederacy, was on a winning streak against the armies of the United States of the Union. At the battle of Gettysburg, in Pennsylvania, the Confederate armies outnumbered the Union soldiers barricading themselves inside the town. General Lee created battle tactics and strategies for the assault on Gettysburg. Through his extensive planning and military genius, Robert E. Lee was confident that his battalions would overtake the Union. However, during this decisive battle, Robert E. Lee's strategies failed the Confederacy, and the unexpected happened; Ulysses S. Grant and the Union armies defeated Lee. Even though General Lee planned thoroughly, Lee did not expect the Union to retreat to Cemetery Hill where they would have the advantage of elevation. Both sides suffered major casualties, but it was the Union that won the battle.

Comments: Very colorful depiction of the Civil War with excellent detail, in particular the notion that "Lee did not expect the Union to retreat to Cemetery Hill where they would have the advantage of elevation."

Columbus

Annie L — In the 1400s, the majority of Europeans believed that the world was flat. However, a small group of people had a theory that the world was round. With the help of Queen Isabella, a young man named Christopher Columbus put together a team of explorers. In hopes of finding a new trade route to China, these ambitious men boarded their boats and set sail. Instead of finding asia, Columbus and his crew stumbled upon a new land; America. Columbus discovered a whole new continent. Furthermore, he proved to Europeans that the world was actually round. With his endurance, intelligence, and creativity, Columbus and his crew discovered the continent of North America.

Comments: This paragraph is an excellent example of variety in sentence structure. Notice how Annie leads into her main sentences with complex and varied openings such as: "*With the help of Queen Isabella*, a young man named Christopher Columbus put together a team of explorers. *In hopes of finding a new trade route to China*, these ambitious men boarded their boats and set sail. *Instead of finding asia*, Columbus and his crew stumbled upon a new land; America. Columbus discovered a whole new continent. *Furthermore*, he proved to Europeans that the world was actually round. *With his endurance, intelligence, and creativity,* Columbus and his crew discovered the continent of North America." The mark of a very sophisticated and elegant writer.

Renaissance

Amanda C — The Renaissance, the rebirth of new ideas throughout 14th century Europe underlines the idea of how sucessful creativity can be. Once burdened with the threat of the deadly Black Death plague, people of the 1300s began to think differently about the world. Italy, the cradle of life for the Renaissance, was the first to introduce new concepts of philosophy, art, and human thinking. Instead of being concerned about the spiritual aspects of life, the population began to focus on material possessions. In addition, art became more lifelike and famous artists that society still reveres today, like Leonardo da Vinci, emerged. With the help of the Renaissance, Europe was able to break free of the Middle Ages and entered a new era, an era of creativity and uniqueness.

Comments: Beautiful writing, excellent historical description, terrific concluding sentence.

Harriet Tubman

Jess A — Compelling illustration that imagination is essential to society's advancement is demonstrated by the Underground Railroad. Harriet Tubman, a former slave, guided three hundred slaves to freedom using a network of people and resources coordinated in secrecy. As a "conductor", she risked her life while completing nineteen trips to the South during the end of the 18th century. In order to avoid danger, Tubman suggested that the slaves travel during the night. Imagination was pivotal to the process of freeing the slaves. Tubman used her master's horse and buggy after nightfall, and started the journey on a Saturday night because the paper would not be printed until Monday mornings, so news of the slave's disappearance could not be reported. Without Tubman's creative escape techniques, they would not have completed the journey unscathed.

Comments: The description is so vivid in this paragraph, the writing so fluid, that you almost feel like you were there with Harriet on the "horse and buggy after nightfall". Way to go, Jess, you make history read like a novel.

South Africa

Nick D — The most compelling heroes are always those who use a non violent means to spark a revolution. Thus, Apartheid activist Stephen Biko stands up as one of the most important heroes the dejected continent of Africa has ever known. Biko founded the influential Black Consciousness Movement, where he would speak out against the forces being put against his people. Yet, in a tragic act of martyrdom, Biko was brutally murdered under police custody, which sparked a worldwide glance at whether the Apartheid regime could be trusted. Though Biko is vastly more appreciated posthumously than he was when he was alive, he nonetheless stands as a figurehead of hope for the poverty and violence ridden African nation.

Comments: Super writing with excellent transitions. Notice how Nick uses "Thus", "Yet" and "Nonetheless" to control the direction of the narrative.

Nelson Mandela

Rachel H — During the late 1980s and throughout the 90s, in a time of major strife and conflict in South Africa, Nelson Mandela worked against the common opinion of his country and became a beaker of peace, and resolution. In a time of great hate and tension between blacks and whites, Mandela went against the majority to unify his country. He was an active anti-apartheid activist and was initially committed to non-violence resistance. Though, the South African court convicted him on charges of sabotage, as well as other crimes committed while he led the movement against the apartheid. Mandela served 27 years in prison in accordance to the charges placed against him. Despite spending so many years in confinement, Mandela went on to become the president of South Africa in 1994. However, he inherited a country where the majority opinion was hatred and anger. He realized that he must take a separate path; to become a symbol of unity and to build a bridge between the two colors. When he became elected president in 1994, he used a white sporting event (the Rugby World Cup) as an excuse to bring together the entire nation. He encouraged young black men to cheer on the white, South African rugby players during the World Championships, which was held in South Africa. Mandela separated himself from the views of the nation and used his positive morale to create a better nation that works to expel hatred instead of promoting it.

Comments: By now, many of you may recognize the basis for the movie *Invictus*. But Rachel wrote this well in advance of the movie's premiere, providing great sociological insight into the life and times of Mandela. And great historical depth. After reading this, who needs to see the movie.

Somali Pirates

Katrina K — Finally, a modern example of originality at work occurred just this past April during a hijacking attempt by Somali pirates. An American ship, the Maersk Alabama, was sailing from the United States bringing relief aid to Kenya when it was intercepted by armed Somali pirates. Rather than giving into the pirates' demands and joining over 20 other ships from various countries taken hostage by the pirates in 2009, the 20-man crew and Captain Richard Phillips decided to fight back. When dealing with issues of survival, the capacity for originality in the human mind is incredible. The unarmed crew fought off Somali pirates with machine guns by utilizing ship tools and finally locking themselves in the engine room in order to maintain control of the ship. Later in a sticky hostage situation involving Capt. Phillips, the U.S. Marines cleverly come up with new ideas to negotiate with the pirates and trick them into a dead end, saving the captain and crew.

Comments: Such is Katrina's literary expertise that this paragraph, ripped from today's headlines, reads like a made-for-TV-movie. Lots of drama, lots of detail, two key characteristics of excellent SAT essays.

SALT I and II

Griffin B — The importance of ethics needed to work towards the common good is also shown through the strategic initiative utilized during the Cold War. After WWII the world was on the brink of nuclear war. The United States and the Soviet Union had been contradictory allies since the formation of the Soviet Union during WWI in the Bolshevik revolution. The Soviet Union and the United States were however able to avoid direct fighting through means of ethical behavior. Conferences of SALT I and II and several other arms reductions conferences helped to stem the growing tensions of the Cold War. Leaders like Gorbachev and Nixon, despite their views towards the other nations, initiated in negotiations to avoid the loss of life. This use of ethical behavior in a time of surmounting tensions saved the lives of millions, and ensured the unfaltering progression of a world society.

Comments: Nice description of the political tensions surrounding the Cold War. Good historical insight and analysis as well, particularly in the description of the United States and the Soviet Union as "contradictory allies".

Hitler

Jac G— Another example of greatness of creativity in history is during World War II. When Hitler gained control of Germany, he began to use his power to influence society in the worst of ways. He found a scapegoat for all of the problems Germany and the rest of Europe were having after World War I and amongst a few other minorities, targeted the Jewish people. By doing so, he began to lock them up in concentration camps where they were kept to work for a while and then viciously murdered by gas showers, cremation, shot and all sorts of other terrible ways. In fact, by 1942 over 4 million European Jews had been placed in concentration camps and 3.5 million of those had been murdered. By the end of the war in 1945, 6 million Jews had been killed and most of the ones left had lost their family members during this devastating war. However the ones that survived were seen as the innovative and brilliant people in the eyes of Jews and the rest of the world. To escape terrible death and torture, these people must have been valuable and brilliant thinkers to get themselves out of that kind of situation. More specifically, Elie Wiesel, author of *Night*, was willing to share his story with the rest of the world, proving to be one of the most creative thinkers of this time. He believed that we can only try and prevent history from repeating itself if we learn all the facts from previous times and with the help of his novel, Wiesel was seen as a figure of hope in the Jewish community as well as the rest of the world.

Comments: Excellent writing in this very detailed depiction of Hitler's brutality. Nice transitions and subordination throughout. Very fluid writing style.

Japanese Intenment Camps

Nicole T — One fascinating example that creative individuals are needed in society is Fred Korematsu's protest against the internment of Japanese Americans. With FDR issuing Executive Order 9066 after the bombing of Pearl Harbor, all Japanese Americans were forced to move to internment camps. Knowing the order was a direct violation of individual rights, Korematsu evaded internment. He was arrested later on for disobeying the law. By taking his case to the Supreme Court, Korematsu decided to fight against the blatant racism against Japanese Americans. Not only did Korematsu attempt to overcome racial discrimination, but also gain equal rights for Japanese Americans. Although the Supreme Court ruled against the case, Korematsu v. United States demonstrated the racism involved in the unfair treatment of Japanese Americans during World War II. However, Korematsu's courage and creativity lives on forever and reminds us to eliminate racial discrimination and preserve equality.

Comments: This paragraph highlights a little-known episode in the lives of Japanese Americans during the Second World War. Notice the attention to detail; Nicole not only mentions the decree order signed by FDR, but also the Supreme Court case that "demonstrated the racism involved in the unfair treatment of Japanese Americans."

John Adams

Ashley S —The idea of creative minds fueling progress is exemplified by president John Adam's trip to France in 1773. The United States was losing their battle for independence from Britain and the military needed the support of any who could help. In a desperate, and what many deemed "hopeless", attempt to gain a powerful ally, Adams sailed to France to meet with Benjamin Franklin and Arthur Lee, where they hoped to forge an alliance with France. Adams immersed himself in French culture, learning the language, attending the theatre, and befriending many dignitaries. Eventually, he met with 24 year old, Louis XIV who, after much persuasion, agreed to form an alliance. If Adams had not been so creative and gone to France, the United States may not have won their independence from Britain because of their poor military.

Comments: Excellent description of Adams' attempts to "forge an alliance" with France in this very detailed paragraph. Nice parallel structure when Ashley says: "Adams immersed himself in French culture, learning the language, attending the theatre, and befriending many dignitaries."

Personal Experience

I include a wide variety of examples here in order to help you get off the ground running with your compositions; just remember that readers give higher marks to students who use external examples from history, literature, science and art. Personal experience is low man on the College Board totem pole. Use it if you must, but in general be sure to include two other paragraphs with external examples as well.

In this section, the following personal experience topics are covered by student writers in content examples to support various topics:

- Trip to Yosemite
- Typhoid Patients
- Camp Carnival
- Katrina Relief Effort
- Fixer Upper
- Drama Club
- Rube Goldberg
- Handicapped Horseback Riding
- Amigos
- Community Service
- Escape from Iran

Trip to Yosemite

Kent H — A third illustration of the notion that plans can always go wrong is seen through my experiences in the Boy Scouts of America. Last summer, I led a thirty-mile backpack trip through the Yosemite Valley. For months prior to the trip, I planned out the schedules, meals, equipment, parent volunteers, and path that we would follow. As the trip approached, I was confident that it was going to be a great success as a result of all of the planning that I had done in advance. However, on the morning of the trip something went extremely wrong. One of the father chaperones didn't show up because he thought that the trip was a week later than it actually was. Consequently, the number of adult leaders on the trek was cut down by one and the number of drivers that would take us to our starting point was reduced. We made do with one less supervisor, but the miscommunication had resulted in serious setbacks.

Comments: Overall this paragraph exhibits a wide variety of sentence structure and excellent transitions. Notice the way Kent uses an introductory phrase or clause as a prelude to almost all of his sentences. For example: *"For months prior to the trip*, I planned out the schedules, meals, equipment, parent volunteers, and path that we would follow. *As the trip approached*, I was confident that it was going to be a great success as a result of all of the planning that I had done in advance." This sort of subordination is the mark of an excellent writer. Also, I really like the way Kent ends his story with the phrase "resulted in serious setbacks". It's an elegant and sophisticated phrase to use in place of the more mundane "shit happens." Keep it in your Bag of Tricks.

Camp Carnival

Colleen M — A final example of planning being effected by an unpredictable occurrence happened in my own personal experience with a camp carnival. As the leader of the camps' events for the month of June, I created the idea of a carnival, complete with entertainment, games, and lunch. After months of detailed planning including invitations, entertainment, refreshments, food, and setup, I could not wait for the exciting day. Although the date was especially picked after examining the weather, there is no counting on Mother Nature. After a wonderful and entire hour into the carnival, the sky became cloudy and drops of water began to fall. Although I was disappointed, I learned that due to the unexpected, even regarding the most detailed plans, there is nothing that guarantees the perfect execution of such a plan.

Comments: Colleen may have studied Kent's personal experience paragraph before she wrote her own. If she did, great; if she didn't, great. In any case her sentence structure is just as varied and sophisticated as Kent's. Check out her subordination: *As the leader of the camps' events for the month of June, I created the idea of a carnival, complete with entertainment, games, and lunch. After months of detailed planning including invitations, entertainment, refreshments, food, and setup, I could not wait for the exciting day. Although the date was especially picked after examining the weather, there is no counting on Mother Nature. "* Also, I really like that last bit about the vagaries of Mother Nature. Excellent writing.

Typhoid Patients

Jonathan W — A final example of the need for creativity to achieve progress is through my personal experience working with typhoid patients in Southeast Asia last summer. A few of my friends and I shadowed a team of

UNICEF doctors that brought clean water to those villages especially hard hit by typhoid and ebola. Although there were limited supplies for each village that we visited, the team and the local villagers worked to find creative solutions to keeping the drinking water clean, such as building makeshift sewage systems as well as making treatment from the native plants in the area for afflicted patients. Through our fresh ideas and determination to keep the terrible diseases from spreading, hundreds of lives were saved and the village had enough working people to begin producing more than they ever had before. These small secluded populations were able to make progress despite receiving little government aid because of the innovative ideas that the UNICEF team and the villagers had created.

Comments: Jonathan travels to Africa -- entirely in his imagination, as he told me later -- to construct a compelling account of the plight of Southeast Asians "hard hit by typhoid and ebola". You, too, can travel to foreign lands to help out humanity in your SAT essay. Remember what Einstein said: "Imagination is more important than knowledge."

Katrina Relief Effort

Grace W — Lastly, creativity was very important in a recent personal experience of my own. A few years ago I traveled to New Orleans to help with the Hurricane Katrina relief effort. I remember mentally preparing myself by imagining a city so broken down that it would take years to fix. Yet, when I actually arrived in New Orleans, I realized that none of the images I had created in my mind came close to the horror that was laid out in front of me. During my two weeks in New Orleans, creative ideas were needed constantly. We had to brainstorm ways to rescue people out of teeny crevices and think of words that would make terrified people feel at ease. I learned that in any situation where people are scared out of their minds, creativity is necessary in trying to calm them down and in trying to make them feel more comfortable.

Comments: This pet paragraph blew me away. The writing is so vivid and the detail so emphatic, I actually "believed" that Grace had travelled to New Orleans to help with the Katrina effort. Of course, the experience was entirely imaginary; Grace only assisted in the relief effort *in her head*. But, as far as SAT Readers are concerned, it doesn't matter. It's the writing that matters, not whether the material is real or imaginary.

Fixer Upper

Mallory L — In my own personal experience, creativity has ensued progress. This past summer, my mother and I fixed up our rental property in Oakland, California , to make it rentable. From a leaky toilet to peeling lead paint on an overhang to a one hundred year old oven that had not been cleaned in 25 years, we had to put our heads together to create cheap solutions to these problems, because we were on a tight budget. After brainstorming for a while, my mother and I decided to bend the float lever on the toilet, which kept the water level down, scrape off the lead paint, dispose of it, and spray grey primer on it, to cover up the rusty metal, and use CLR, or Calcium, Lime, Rust remover on the oven. After sixteen hours of cleaning and fixing up, we had a quaint little house, ready to be occupied. Because we came up with creative solutions, progress followed; we rented out the house.

Comments: I love Mallory's extremely detailed description of her summer work on the rental property. She uses phrases like "leaky toilet and peeling lead paint" and employs parallel structure (verbs in italics) to excellent effect, as in: ". . . my mother and I decided to *bend* the float lever on the toilet, which kept the water level down, *scrape* off the lead paint, *dispose* of it, and *spray* grey primer on it, to cover up the rusty metal, and *use* CLR.

Drama Club

Hillary M — A final depiction of false impressions derived from image occurred in my own personal experience with a school play. As a member of my school's drama club, I shared the task of putting on the spring musical. My job was to scout talented, outgoing kids as possible actors and actresses. An acquaintance of mine, Derrick, was a soft-spoken basketball player who mostly kept to himself. Because of his quiet demeanor and jock reputation, I assumed Derrick would not be interested in the play and did not bother inviting him to the auditions. However, I was incredibly surprised when he attended anyway, and gave a fantastic audition showcasing theatrical abilities no one knew he had. From that experience, I learned the meaning of the old proverb "You can't judge a book by its cover."

Comments: An excellent paragraph full of important detail. Hillary varies her sentence structure and introduces her subject, Derrick, with journalistic touches: "An acquaintance of mine, Derrick, was a *soft-spoken* basketball player who *mostly kept to himself*. Because of his *quiet demeanor and jock reputation . . .*". This puts the reader in the room with the character. Also, Hillary closes with a nice quote and makes sure to mention what she *learned* from the experience. Excellent writing.

Rube Goldberg

Miles G — A third illustration of the notion that our advances succumb to losses can be seen in my personal experience. For my final 8th grade science project, I was teamed up with four other boys and assigned to build a Rube Goldberg machine. Rube Goldberg made intricately complicated contraptions to perform menial tasks. My group decided to build a machine to place a stamp on a letter. We made many advances in devising our machine and drawing up the specifications for it. We thought that our contraption would receive first place and that we would finish early. Yet in the end, due to personal disagreements and calculation errors, our project lost points and did not turnout or perform like we hoped it would.

Comments: This is excellent writing, particularly in such sentences as: "Rube Goldberg made intricately complicated contraptions to perform menial tasks." Miles tells an engaging personal story here and throws in a nice transition to point out exactly what went wrong with the project: "Yet in the end, due to personal disagreements and calculation errors, our project lost points and did not turnout or perform like we hoped it would." Good stuff.

Handicapped Horseback Riding

Aliyah S — A third illustration of the idea that plans often go wrong can be seen through my experiences as a volunteer worker for a handicapped horseback riding ranch. Last year, we began planning our annual horse show four months in advance. The children had been practicing for weeks. The volunteers had spent hours weeding, painting the barn, planting new flowers, and decorating the arena. However, two days before the show, something completely unexpected happened. The weatherman on TV called for rainshowers - in July! Consequently, the show was delayed for two weeks. Despite a reduced amount of participants due to family vacations that had been previously planned, the show was a relative success, although late.

Comments: Excellent writing with good parallel sentence structure. Notice how Aliyah stacks up her verbs when she says: "The volunteers had spent hours *weeding*, *painting* the barn, *planting* new flowers, and *decorating* the arena." Also note her use of the surprise interjection "- in July!", which gives the paragraph unexpected drama. Nice.

Amigos

Brian W — A third illustration of the notion that the aspirations of a group always exceed the goals of an individual is seen through my experiences in Mexico with the community service group known as Amigos. Last summer I was a volunteer in the program Amigos in which I traveled to Oaxaca to live, help, and rebuild the community of the less fortunate. After months of preparation learning Spanish, studying the culture, and fundraising, the date of my trip to the hot Oaxaca came. In an effort to improve the lives of the inhabitants in my community, I did all I could to help and teach the families I lived with. One day out of the rest seems to lay in my memory. After a long day's work until four o'clock in the afternoon, I was tired and exhausted from rebuilding latrines in my community. About an hour later, I was approached by one of the residents who asked if I could continue working for a group of the men who wanted to finish the latrine before the day's end. Although I knew I was worn-out, I put mind over matter and agreed to help out. By the time we finished it was about eight o'clock, however the newly found feeling of self-content was outstanding. For me, the lesson to be learned was to put the selfish individual needs aside and be a team player.

Comments: This paragraph is similar in theme to the one we saw in the sample essay in Chapter 2, although somewhat longer. I include it as an example of a personal experience that takes up roughly half the length of a typical essay. Clocking in at around 220 words, it's full of psychological insight — "Although I knew I was worn-out, I put mind over matter and agreed to help out." — and social conscience: "For me, the lesson to be learned was to put the selfish individual needs aside and be a team player." If you are going to use personal experience to chew up space on the SAT essay, this is the way to do it.

Community Service

Amanda M — A final illustration of the notion that plans may go wrong is seen through my experiences in my community service group. Last spring I was head of the entertainment and activities committee in the Moraga Youth Involvement Committee. We decided that it would be fun to plan a movie night featuring, The *Incredibles*, in the Moraga Commons Park on a weekend in late May. As a group we began planning the event early March gathering donations for the concession stand, finding a projection screen and sound system, and making sure that our event was publicized well to gather a promising crowd. Everything was in order and ready to go the day of the event when my commissioner received a phone call from an employee from Disney. The Disney employee explained that in order to show a film produced by Disney we needed to sign a $500 release form two weeks prior to the event. Unfortunately we had been unaware of the form and were forced to cancel the event. Even though we were certain that the event was a sure success, we skipped a very important detail in order to make the night become a reality.

Comments: Amanda deals with real-world economic problems in this paragraph and includes an impressive amount of detail. Good variety of sentence structure and use of transitions. I also like how she starts out using "I" but quickly broadens the scope of the paragraph to "we". Nice way to expand a personal experience paragraph to encompass the world at large.

Escape from Iran

Kimi A — A final illustration that progress is not possible without sacrifice occurred in my own personal experience. My grandmother is one of the strongest women I know today. In her day, she sacrificed a tremendous amount for her family to be safe, secure, and happy. In the late 1970's, the revolution in Iran placed many people in a dangerous environment, many serving under harsh governmental forces, and others fleeing the country. My grandmother and her family, being one of those lucky families who could escape before time was no longer on their side. With hardships entering the U.S. and a small amount of money with her, my grandmother made the best of what she had, and became a successful lawyer in the United States. She raised her three children to be come successful people themselves, not only in their careers, but also in their happiness as well. The sacrifice she made improved the lives of her children, grandchildren, and many generations yet to come.

Comments: Lots of global sweep in this personal experience. You really get a sense of history, culture, and sacrifice reading Kimi's paragraph. Good parallel structure ("she sacrificed a tremendous amount for her family to be safe, secure, and happy"), variety of sentence strtucture and transitions. Plus, it's all true. Or so it seems. But what if Kimi actually made it all up? Well, she didn't, but what's to stop you from making up your own personal experience involving a fictious grandmother? Nothing at all. Remember, the essay is a work of fact plus fiction. Have fun inventing the personal experience of your choice. Once again, remember: "Imagination is more important than knowledge."

8—Spin the Prompt

Appearances don't always reflect reality. The sun, for example, does not revolve around the earth. The race is not always to the swift. There's no such thing as centrifugal force. Glass is actually a liquid. And milk doesn't really do a body good.

So it is with the SAT prompt. What you see is not necessarily what you get. Every SAT prompt, no matter what it *seems* to be asking, can always be spun, or interpreted, to your advantage.

Recall (from Chapter 5, *Real Essays*) the prompt presented in the October 2005 SAT:

> **prompt**: Is society's admiration for famous people beneficial or harmful?

Rather than define famous people as powder-puff celebrities appearing on Letterman or Oprah, Alex S took famous people to mean social and literary role models. This enabled her to reach into her Bag of Tricks and pull out content examples on historical heavyweights like Martin Luther King and Elizabeth Cady Stanton. Hester Prynne was the obvious choice for a literary heroine.

In April, 2006, Tara T. was presented with what at first glance looked like a completely different prompt:

> **prompt**: Is our ability to change ourselves unlimited or are there limits on our ability to make important changes in our lives?

Tara spun this prompt to her advantage by simply focusing on individuals who produced change in society: MLK, Susan B, and Hester Prynne. Important point: notice that you don't have to address the prompt in its entirety. Simply choose to argue a position on one side of the "or".

The May, 2006, prompt asked:

> **prompt**: Does the truth change depending on how people look at things?

In this case, Alaizah K. took the prompt at face value and simply defined truth as something that differs depending on a person's perspective. She then reached into her Bag of Tricks and pulled out content examples relating to the Civil War (racial perspective), William Randolph Hearst (journalistic perspective) and Jay Gatsby (perspective on the American dream). Truth, in other words, is in the eye of the beholder.

In some sense, all SAT prompts boil down to a fairly simple premise: Drama. Show how some obstacle was overcome, some challenge met, some struggle resolved. That's it. No matter how the prompt is worded, no matter how many extraneous quotations are presented in the prompt box, it all comes down to showing how individuals grappled with problems that were eventually resolved, either by the group or the individual or both.

As we've seen, it's fairly easy to come up with a variety of social, historical, cultural, technological or personal content examples to use as supporting examples. Civil Rights, in particular, can be used as a wild card for most SAT essays. It's hard to imagine a more appropriate card to play in this game of revolving topics than Martin Luther King, whose Civil Rights anthem encapsulates the basic premise of virtually every SAT prompt: We shall overcome.

And overcome we shall. By now you're well acquainted with the basics of SAT essay writing. You know how to:

- Set up interesting introductions and conclusions with supporting quotes/anecdotes
- Construct content examples involving history, literature, pop culture, technology and personal experience
- Employ transitions, both within and between paragraphs
- And last but not least -- *spin the prompt* to define your topic sentence

Interpretation

As we saw in Tara's take on the "ability to change ourselves" prompt on the previous page, you don't have to address the prompt in its entirety. Presented with an either/or prompt, you just have to pick a side and support it. What matters more than the prompt itself is your interpretation of the prompt.

Take note: I'm not suggesting that you ignore the prompt and write off topic -- the college board will either give you a zero for the essay or (worse case scenario) withhold your score while they "investigate" your essay. Bad news in either case. Instead, I advise students to interpret (spin) whatever prompt they're given to correspond with the content examples (content examples) they have pre-fabricated in their Bag of Tricks. To summarize:

It's not the prompt itself that's important; it's your interpretation of the prompt that you get judged on.

As long as you handle some part of the prompt, not necessarily the entire prompt itself, your essay is OK. You can, in other words, ignore sections of the prompt that either don't interest you or don't easily conform to your pre-fabricated paragraphs. Take the following prompt, for example:

prompt: Are people better at making observations, discoveries, and decisions if they remain neutral and impartial?

Most kids think they have to addresss all aspects of this prompt, which would be impossible in 25 minutes. Nothing could be further from the truth. I tell my students to pare the prompt down by choosing one of the following -- observations, discoveries OR decisions -- and run with it. Choosing "decisions" is probably the easiest way to go. Since history, literature, music, movies, sports, art, science and pop culture are filled with decisive people, kidz can easily reach into their Bag of Tricks for appropriate content examples. Students, in other words, are not locked into a literal interpretation of the prompt; they are free to slice and dice the prompt, free to improvise so long as they stay true to the basic message of the prompt.

Students handle the second part of the prompt -- neutral and impartial -- by saying individuals make decisions from their heart, from the courage of their convictions, from their passionate idealism, etc. etc. The vast majority of prompts given by the college board can be handled in this manner.

Sample Prompts

To reinforce this point, I include some sample prompts below taken from various SAT exams over the last few years. I follow each of the prompts with a brief description of the suggested spin. The spin is intentionally brief, since you will see many of these same prompts handled in full-length essays in the next chapter, *Go Fish*.

≡

Note: The College Board periodically publishes these prompts after exams are scored. In addition many websites post complete lists of prompts for interested students. One of the best of these is: http://www.onlinemathlearning.com/sat-test-prep.html

prompt: Do society and other people benefit when individuals pursue their own goals?

Spin: What sort of people pursue their own goals? Decisive people, people with vision, people with passion -- in other words, all sorts of individuls many of whom are in history, literature, music, movies, sports, art, science and pop culture. Reach into your Bag of Tricks and pull out content examples on individuals like FDR, Ghandi, Hester Prynne, Lady Gaga, Jackie Robinson, Einstein, Taylor Swift, or someone from your personal experience.

prompt: Is it better for people to stop trying when they feel certain they will not succeed?

Spin: This is a real prompt; I kid you not. What kind of people refuse to stop trying? What kind of people never give up? Simply reach into your Bag of Tricks and select content examples of persistent people in history, literature, music, movies, sports, art, science and pop culture.

prompt: Do highly accomplished people achieve more than others mainly because they expect more of themselves?

Spin: What kind of people expect more of themselves? People who have made a name for themselves in history, literature, music, movies, sports, art, science and pop culture. Huck Finn, Tom Joad from the Grapes of Wrath, Odysseus, Abraham Lincoln, Frodo, Tupac Shakur, Stephanie Meyer, and so on.

prompt: Is striving to achieve a goal always the best course of action, or should people give up if they are not making progress?

Spin: This is a real but ridiculous prompt. What kind of people never give up? Persistent people, decisive people, courageous people, innovative people. Reach into your Bag of Tricks and pull out content examples of such people to populate your essay and support the topic.

prompt: Does progress depend on people with new ideas rather than on people whose ideas are based on the traditional way of doing things?

Spin: Progress depends on people who come up with new ideas. People like Picasso, Galileo, Harriet Tubman, Randall McMurphy (from Cuckoo's Nest) Mark Zuckerburg, Ender Wiggin (from Ender's game), Eminem and so on. Reach into your Bag of Tricks and pull out appropriate content examples. You can slice and dice the prompt to ignore the part about doing things the traditional way.

prompt: Do memories hinder or help people in their effort to learn from the past and succeed in the present?

Spin: It would be nice to simply interpret this prompt as dealing with success, but that might be stripping it too close to the bone. You're gonna have to include memories in your spin. Best to handle this by using content examples that build on events from the past. MLK, for example, took his ideas of non-violence from Ghandi. Rappers "sample" riffs from previous artists. Picasso built on but eventually deviated from the work of the Impressionists. *Twilight* is simply a new look at an old obsession. Stuff like that. A great quote to use for this prompt would be a slight variation on the quote from Santayana we saw in Chapter 6 ("Quotes"): *Those who don't remember the past are forever forced to repeat it.* Also, the quotes in the *Context* page at the front of this book all resonate with this theme.

prompt: Is the effort involved in pursuing any goal valuable, even if the goal is not reached?

Spin: This assignment is difficult ONLY if you look at the whole sentence. If you lop off the last part ("even if the goal is not reached") the prompt becomes easy. What kind of people consider the pursuit of goals valuable? Virtually everybody in history, literature, music, movies, sports, art, science and pop culture. Remember, you can interpret and/or slice-and-dice the prompt any way you want in order to keep your pencil moving and fill up two pages of white space.

prompt: Is society's admiration for famous people beneficial or harmful?

Spin: Remember how Alex handled this prompt in the beginning of this chapter (and back in Chapter 5 Real Essays). She stated that famous people are role models, then simply went on to describe the activities that made them famous, using MLK, Suffragets and Hester Prynne. Slam dunk.

prompt: Is a person responsible, through the example he or she sets, for the behavior of other people?

Spin: At first glance, this prompt might be considered difficult. However, once you realize that it can be addressed with "role models" (as we just saw in the previous prompt), you fall back on people whose activities in history, literature, sports, art, science and pop culture were noteworthy for society.

prompt: Is solitude—spending time alone—necessary for people to achieve their most important goals?

Spin:If you imagine the prompt is about solitude, then this topic could be daunting. On the other hand, if you realize this prompt is really about goals, then you are back in business. What kind of people pursue goals, whether in public or in solitude? Creative people. Remember, don't let the prompt overpower you. It's your interpretation of the prompt rather than the prompt itself that matters.

prompt: Are the values of a society most clearly revealed in its popular culture?
Spin: The topic here can be reduced to popular culture. Use content examples from movies, music, art, TV, sports and so on to show how they reflect the values of society. Might be fun to use reality TV (*Keeping up with the Kardashians*) as an example of social values run amuk!

prompt: Is there any value for people to belong only to a group or groups with which they have something in common?
Spin: At first glance, this prompt is so simultaneously vague AND obvious as to be anxiety-provoking. But relax. Don't lose any time worrying about what the College Board has in mind here. Simply state that innovative, decisive, and progressive people thrive in a group context and then use content examples from your Bag of Tricks to support this contention.

prompt: Should people make more of an effort to keep some things private?
Spin: This is very similar to the previous prompt. Since creative people tend to be public people -- and since we live in a free and open society (well, that's what the schools say, anyway) -- the best way to handle this prompt is to take your content examples public. Who needs privacy? Not innovative, decisive people. Even guys like Einstein, who started off a recluse in a Swiss patent office, eventually end up public figures.

prompt: Does everyone need a family or a network to survive?
Spin: Most interesting people (the kind of people in your Bag of Tricks!) thrive in a group environment. Translate "network" as "group" and fall back on examples of individuals doing socially productive work or work that occured in a group context. For example: Atticus Finch in *Mockingbird*, Spiderman, the Beatles, Facebook, Barak Obama, Schindler from *Schindler's War*, Henry Ford, Katrina relief effort, etc. etc.

prompt: Do people tend to get along better with people who are very different from them or with those who are like them?
Spin: Best strategy here is to state that people work best with groups of like-minded people, people who they can bounce their ideas off of. Musicians, athletes, political leaders, scientists, artists, religious leaders, writers, actors, and directors all need an "audience" that appreciates their work or rallies around their viewpoints. Reach into your Bag of Tricks and pull out appropriate examples.

Couple of Toughies

As we've seen, SAT prompts are usually pretty generic and can be handled quickly and easily as long as you have prefabricated content examples drawn from one or more of the following: history, literature, movies, music, sports, art, science, popular culture and personal experience. All things considered, by now you should feel pretty confident in your ability to handle all possible prompts with intelligence and insight.

Sometimes, however, the college board throws a curve ball at you.

This section presents two prompts that represent a couple of topics more difficult than those we've seen previously because their scope is more narrowly defined. Following each prompt is an essay which demonstrates how to spin even a difficult prompt.

prompt: Do people put too much emphasis on learning practical skills?

Examples used:

- FDR and the New Deal as a practical way for government to help people out of poverty
- Personal experience, importance of taking responsibility for one's actions
- *Catcher in the Rye* — Holden starts off childish but learns responsibility and grows up along the way

Nicole H., June 2005 essay (score = 11)

From the day someone is born, they are taught new concepts everyday. Some skills may be useful later on in life and others are just plain nonsense. Although many people disregard what others have taught them, it is necessary to obtain such basic skills in order to live life to its full potential. Our world, and its people would not be where they are today without the practical skills that have been used.

Franklin D Roosevelt exemplified the importance of practicality during his presidency. He entered into office during a time of a great depression and low morale of the American people. In order to remove America from this horrific phase, he enabled his practical skills and created the New Deal. The New Deal created programs such as the Social Security Act and the Fair Labor Standards Act which led Americans to realize how important practical things are in life. FDR presented the idea that the easiest skill to obtain is patriotism for the United States and that was fully accomplished with the New Deal. FDR was a very practically based president and ultimately led America in the right direction.

The use of practical skills can also be found in everyday life. Ever since I was a child, I was taught to be responsible. My mother told me that this was a necessary skill and that it would benefit me later on in life. So, I would always take out the garbage, clean my room and finish my homework. In my freshman year, I was nominated and elected to be a part of my school's leadership because I was such a responsible student. The practical skill of responsibility led me into an activity that I still enjoy participating in today.

An example of practicality within literature is Holden Caughfield in *The Catcher in the Rye*. Holden's desire for childhood is caused by his inability to perform complicated tasks in the adult world. Childhood is full of innocence and easy decision making and Holden never wanted to leave this realm due to fear and low confidence. Holden is taught practical skills in the book and eventually makes the most difficult choice of all and that is to grow up.

Practical skills can lead many people to success if they are used in the correct way. It is our decision if we want to use what we have learned and live to our fullest potential.

prompt: Do changes that make our life easier necessarily make them better?

Examples used:

- Slavery made the lives of southern whites easier but not necessarily better in terms of democratic ideals
- The Internet makes access to information easier but also makes users more vulnerable to identity theft and chat-room stalkers
- Fast foods are convenient but lack nutrition and prevent traditional dinner table conversation

Hillary M (practice essay)

Since the Industrial Revolution of the 1800s, Americans have sought to improve their lives through new inventions. Eli Whitney's cotton gin, Henry Ford's Model T, and the du Pont family's cellulose-based film did in fact provide positive change that made the lives of countless people easier. However, changes that make our lives easier do not necessarily make them better. This universal truth is exemplified throughout history, technology, and modern culture.

The dark side of life improvements can be seen in the example of slavery in the United States. When early Americans began exploiting the African race during the beginning of the eighteenth century, they were pleased to discover that they could accomplish great amounts of work with a work force that not only required no compensation, but that also reproduced itself. While the lives of Southern whites were undeniably made easier, they were certainly not made better in a moral or ethical sense. In addition, denying a people their God-given rights based strictly on race did not make America a better democracy.

Advanced technology serves as another illustration of positive changes that do not necessarily make our lives better. The internet has made millions of peoples' lives significantly less complicated. They can shop online, get driving directions and simulate their social interactions through chat rooms. Unfortunately, the internet has resulted in new dangers in addition to these new features. Numerous people have become victims of identity theft due to personal information leaked on the internet, and women and children are susceptible to sexual predators on internet chat sites. While this invention has made our lives considerably easier, by increasing these risks it has also made our lives less safe.

A final example of change that makes life simpler but not better can be seen in the eating habits of modern society. Today we have vast chains of fast food restaurants such as McDonalds and KFC at our disposal. These establishments cater to our busy agendas by offering cheap and quickly-acquired meals. However, while convenient, fast food is also incredibly unhealthy. In addition to denying our bodies nutritional value, fast food often inadvertently robs families of quality time together by replacing dinner times traditionally spent at home. Fast food may make our lives easier, but it does not necessarily improve the overall quality of our family life.

As we have seen in these examples of history, technology, and modern culture, changes that make our lives easier do not necessarily enhance them for the better. We should be aware of the negative implications that accompany change before we so eagerly embrace it.

No Spin Zone

Every once in a while spin, while possible, may not be necessary. Here, for example, is the prompt from the March, 2011 SAT.

> **prompt**: Are photographs straightforward representations of real life, or are they artistic creations reflecting the photographer's point of view?

Rather than spin this prompt, many of my students simpy addressed it head on, using photographs as seques into their content examples. Check out this essay from a student who received a perfect score.

> Lauren A., March 2011 essay (score = 12)

As the famous photographer Arthur Jones once said, "Photos show the emotion of a specific event." He is stating that without photographs, one would not be able to see how an event was, especially the emotions involved. Throughout history, there have been many pictures taken to depict an event. This will be illustrated through teh Chicano Student walkout in East LA, the battle of Iwo Jima and a personal experience.

In 1964, Mexican American students lead a protest against their East L.A. school district. Many photographs were taken at the event, and they didn't sugar coat anything. The photographs showed the brutality of the force the police were using against harmless students who just wanted their rights. The photographs showed real lifel. They showed the police punching, kicking and threatening the students. The pictures or evidence ultimately led to some policemen getting fired.

In 1944, the valient U.S. troops led a brave and courageous battle in Iwo Jima, Japan. At the time, the Japanese were a brutal, unstoppable force; however, the U.S. troops courageously fought them and ultimately won. The pictures that were taken during the battle of Iwo Jima capture the bloodshed and bravery of all the troops involved. The most famous photograph from Iwo Jima is the picture of the troops raising the American flag on the Japanese soil. The photographs taken at Iwo Jima depict bloodshed, violence and courage, not sugar-coate. General Patton once said, "These pictures showed the strength of the troops."

Lastly, photopgrahs can capture joy, happiness and love. My mom takes pictures of real life events. Last summer, we went to Zimbabwe to help with patients dealing with HIV and AIDS. She captured real life strength, loneliness and love. While we were helping out she asked if she could take pictures and all the patients were OK with it. For some, she captured the last happy memories. The families were very happy she had captured the patient's last few days. One patient said, "Thank you so much for doing this for my family, I want them to remember me forever. It felt great knowing that other people were benefitting from my mom's hobby.

As the famous photographer Leslie Stills, once said, "These pictures seem like frozen moments of real life." Pictures are a moment captured in still life. Many pictures have very nostalgic effects. For some, moments last a couple of minutes but when you have pictures to go along with them then they last forever. Exo dominae. Translated in English, moments can last for life.

Lauren reached into her Bag of Tricks for appropriate content examples and used a photograph as a seque into each. She didn't so much spin the prompt as graft a photograph onto each of her examples. The flag at Iwo Jima was a nice touch. And the student demonstrations at East L.A. made the essay topical. But the kicker was Lauren's trip to Zimbabwe, a compelling and purely fictional excursion into Africa to both bond with her mom and help AIDS patients. Her conclusion is good, if the Latin somewhat shaky.

Remember, the point of the essay is to demonstrate writing ability -- whether or not the events portrayed actually transpired (in whatever language) is beside the point.

Note: In a recent New York Times article, Angela Garcia, executive director of the SAT said, "The primary goal of the essay prompt is to give students an opportunity to demonstrate their *writing* skills." (italics mine)

One Final Twist

Just to keep you on your toes and help you "expect the unexpected", here's an unusual prompt that hasn't yet appeared — though the east coast prompt for the March 2011 test was close — and an equally unusual response. I call it the point/counterpoint essay; it's definitely off the beaten path. For this reason, I don't generally recommend it. Nonetheless, it's a useful strategy to tuck away in your Bag of Tricks for a rainy day. It's also a handy strategy to keep in mind if you decide to take the ACT, where this kind of approach is expected.

Point/Counterpoint Essay

Previously, we've seen many examples of paragraphs with transition words like *however, yet, on the other hand* all of which prepare the reader for the flip side of the argument presented in the first part of the paragraph. Handling this type of point/counterpoint description *within a paragraph* is fairly easy to do.

But employing point/counterpoint technique for *separate paragraphs* is trickier since you typically end up with a four-paragraph instead of a five-paragraph essay, which means you have to invest more time and effort on your intro and conclusion in order to pump up your word count.

So here's a sample prompt followed by a four-paragraph point/counterpoint essay, which I wrote myself. Notice how the introduction and conclusion are longer than usual since the essay only contains four paragraphs.

> **Prompt:** Does television exert a positive or negative influence on today's society?

> Here's your strategy:

- Define television as a means of communication, a window on social events and both a positive and negative force in American culture
- Cite Civil rights as a protest that were televised across the country, sparking positive national debate
- Point out the exposure of young people to TV violence and cite commericals as disruption of narrative flow

Over the last 50 years, the world has become a global village. Events in far-flung places--from China, from Iraq, from Latin America--are presented to Americans every evening on the nightly news. Domestic events of crucial importance from political debates to health-care issues are carried over the public airwaves. In this sense, television serves to inform and educate Americans. However, there's a dark side to TV-watching, especially when it comes to considering its effects on this nation's youth. Consequently, TV in America tends to be a two-edged sword. Television's positive effects are exemplified by the Civil Rights movement in the 1960's, while television's negative effects are illustrated by behavior problems associated with childhood development.

When it comes to race relations, television's effects are largely positive. Television's coverage of the Civil Rights movement in the South, for example, left an indelible image on the minds of many Americans. Shots of black protesters such as Martin Luther King and Jessie Jackson being "hosed down" by white rednecks emphasized and made vivid the racial inequalities that permeated American culture at the time. More recently, TV shows such as the "Cosby Show" and "In Living Color" have helped to bring black culture into the mainstream and mitigate racial prejudice by making Americans more receptive to diverse viewpoints.

On the negative side, however, TV exposes the younger generation to images of violence and mayhem on a daily basis. It's been estimated that children are inundated with up to 157 acts of violence for every six hours of TV viewing. Moreover, Norman Mailer has written that the constant bombardment of commercials disrupts the narrative flow of public TV programs, producing a generation of young adults with short attention span and limited ability to concentrate.

From these examples, it's clear that TV has both beneficial and detrimental effects on Americans, both young and old. When it comes to programs that stress violence and impose commercial interruptions on viewers, TV falls into the category described by Newton Minnow -- a "vast wasteland". However, as a tool for making people aware of historical and political changes in American society, TV is a medium of education and cultural enrichment. It's up to the individual viewer to select programs that emphasize the positive aspects of TV and downplay the negative.

What's Next

This chapter represents the final piece of the SAT essay puzzle. Having read this far, you are now officially a puzzle master. Congratulations. The only thing that remains is to solidify your position as a sophisticated writer. Which means analyzing more examples, written in a variety of styles by a variety of student writers. Which is exactly what the next (and final) chapter — *Go Fish* — provides you ample opportunity to do.

☰

9—Go Fish

Throughout this book, I've stressed the importance of quotes. Well, here's my last one and it's a doozy: *ontogeny recapitulates phylogeny*. Before your eyes glaze over, here's a simple translation of Ernst Haeckel's famous dictum — the evolution of an individual parallels the evolution of the group (or species). An egg, as it grows, passes through the same series of biological forms that its ancestors passed through in evolving to the shape and structure that they have today. Pretty cool. It means we're all connected in a vast, organic web in which each successive part contributes to the next.

Here's a poem of mine, called *Neotony*, that underscores the point:

> Ontogeny recapitulates phylogeny
> Just a fancy way to say
> A not-yet-hairy zygote in a Petri Dish
> Begins life as a fish
> Think that's odd, a little later
> The embryo's an alligator
> What comes next, a horse, a camel?
> Pretty much, in any case a mammal
> Takes the stage and we debate
> The evolution of a tunicate

From this it should be clear to most — Christian Fundamentalists aside — that all life is change and change occurs in stages. Things grow, expand, develop, and evolve, both physically and mentally. You've seen it in your own life. You've seen it in the way I've organized this book. One thing leads to another. You learn how to structure an essay, you learn how to fashion an introduction and conclusion, you learn how to prefabricate transitions and content examples, you learn how to spin the prompt and little by little you put together a logical, cohesive, outstanding SAT essay.

Along the way, you study the patterns that other writers have used to construct their essays. By watching and doing, you learn to vary the forms that came before you and eventually you strike out on your own into original territory.

It's a streamline literary path in some sense analogous to the quote: *ontogeny recapitulates phylogeny*. You've got to crawl before you walk, you've got to walk before you run. And watching other writers is the way to get it done. We all follow in each other's footsteps.

By now it should be clear that I believe that writers evolve through stages, first mimicking the works of others, then slowly developing a voice of their own. Here then, in this final chapter, are dozens of voices of student writers who tackled SAT prompts from a variety of viewpoints, some formulaic, some patently original.

As a final exercise, I want you to read through these essays at your leisure, looking closely at the style and substance of each submission, asking yourself how you would approach the topic, what examples you would use to support your arguments, what quotes you would invoke (or invent!) to advance or summarize the narrative and whether you would stay close to the template presented in this book or invent new forms of your own.

Then sit down with two pages of blank lined paper and practice writing essays based on the prompts included below. Your first essays are openbook and untimed. Later, as your essays get more polished, bring in original material of your own and time yourself for 25 minutes. Keep in mind that top essays require at least 440 words. This translates to roughly 9 words per line, 25 lines per page, two pages total. Test your handwriting out on some lined paper to be sure it's small enough to conform to this stricture.

Then remember, learning by watching and **doing** is the only game in town. So now, take this chapter and go fish. Seriously. Search through the various examples presented here to find essays you like and essays you want to emulate. And then, get busy.

Essays that Work

The following section contains essays from real SATs as well as some practice prompts. All essays have something important going for them, which I point out in the *Comments* section following each piece. These essays are presented in no particular order, although a loose chronology seems to prevail.

Prompt: Does progress depend on people with new ideas rather than on people whose ideas are based on the traditional way of doing things?

Justin S., May 2005 SAT (score = 11)

Franklin D. Roosevelt once said, "The progression of mankind runs parallel to the progression of thought. "His words are still considered valid to this day because throughout history, the world has seen many leaders come and go who have strived for change in society.

The first compelling example of a successful attempt to progress by presenting new ideas is seen through Dr. Martin Luther King Jr. When the young African-American man witnessed social flaws in his life he realized action was vital. Since the current way of confronting the problem wasn't working, he realized the best way to progress was to formulate a new brand of thought. A type that would enlighten people by addressing the current problem of racism and by suggesting that it needed to be dealt with by standing up for their rights. King realized that the progress he desired was only possible if people developed new ideas and concepts. Unfortunately, this great leader was assassinated, but ultimately, his master plan succeeded.

The next example is demonstrated through Nathaniel Hawthorne's epic novel, *The Scarlet Letter*. Protagonist Hester Prynne commits the embarrassing crime of adultery in the beginning of the story. Her partner, reverend Dimmesdale was involved as well. The two decide to handle their problems in different ways. Hester felt she needed to openly apologize, release her feelings publicly, and admit the bare truth. On the other hand, Dimmesdale felt the best way was to keep it in the dark. Hester became a town idol for her honesty, and her malicious partner became mentally distressed. Due to her realization that the past and the current were failing, she threw out new ideas. The town accepted them, and Hester's master plan succeeded as well.

As seen by these two examples, the progress of society does in fact depend on the development of new ideas. Like Roosevelt said, the progression of man runs parallel to the progression of thought.

Comments

I love this essay by Justin for two reasons: (1) Justin was the first of my students to make up quotes and attribute them to some famous figure, in this case FDR. Moreover, his quote nicely encapsulates the theme he pursues in his essay; (2) His paragraph on *The Scarlet Letter* isolates the contrast inherent in the novel, that between light and darkness, between public and private torment. It's a little short, that's true, and one retarded, paint-by-numbers reader gave him a "5" instead of "6", apparently for length. But in my book this essay is golden.

Prompt: Is it better for people to be realistic or optimistic?

Kimi A., December 2006 (score = 12)

Susan Plyte once said "to be optimistic is like carrying oneself with the confidence to be able to achieve anything." Optimistic thinking can benefit anyone with the right mindset. Furthermore, optimism can shape the future of any situation or problem. This universal notion can be exemplified throughout literature, history, and personal experience.

One compelling illustration, demonstrating the benefits of optimism, can be exemplified through John Adler's novel, *The Scarlet Letter*. In this novel, the protagonist, Hester Prynne, has been punished for committing adultery, positioning her in a disgraceful situation. Her punishment is to wear the scarlet letter "A" representing the wrong she has done. However, even with the burden of publicly revealing her shameful mistake, Prynne uses optimistic views by helping out in her community, and bringing out the best values in herself, showing society her exceptional qualities. Her optimism defeated society's ruling upon her, helping her achieve what she strived for.

Another theme that optimistic thinking is beneficial can be illustrated through women's suffrage. From the mid 19 century, women, such as Susan B. Anthony and Elizabeth Cady Stanton, have been publicly campaigning against the lack of rights women had possessed. As early as the Seneca Falls convention in 1848, these women had been looking on the brighter side, imagining a better lifestyle for women all around. With many decades of protests and campaigns, these intellectual and optimistic women have gathered others to rally, make posters, and give innumerable influential speeches around the nation. Not until the 1920's was the 19th amendment passed, guaranteeing woman's right to vote. Without the optimistic views of these bold women, our society today would not be benefiting from the hard work these women did in the past to achieve all this success.

A final illustration that optimistic views produce great achievements is demonstrated through my own personal experience. In the 1970's Iran was having a political revolution, leaving many citizens in danger. However, my grandmother, being one of the lucky handful, thought of an optimistic plan that not only benefited herself, but her family as well. While telling me her unimaginable story, she explained how she had to flee the country before the government could detain her. Her positive thinking got her and her family across safely to the United States, where she later became a successful lawyer. In addition to her success, she was able to send her three children to top of the line schools producing a sharp architect, an intelligent doctor, and my mother, an extremely sophisticated business woman. Without her optimistic thinking, my life wouldn't be as safe and secure as it is today.

As seen through literature, history, and personal experience, optimism can bring a situation a long way, even through stressfully tough adversities. As president JFK stated "Being positive is the key to success."

Comments

Kimi follows in the grand tradition of Alex S., who first used Susan Plyte as a vehicle to introduce a quote appropriate to the prompt. Recall that using a quote (real or imaginary) to spice up your introduction is the way to get the reader on your side from the get go.

Kimi goes on to cite The Scarlet Letter and Women's Rights as two tried-and-true examples of the triumph of optimism. Interestingly, she cited John Adler, rather than Nathaniel Hawthorne, as the author of *The Scarlet Letter*. Since SAT Readers are instructed to ignore inaccuracies in content, she lost no points for this attribution mistake. In fact, I teach my students to make up the name of an author if they have a temporary memory block -- which is exactly what Kimi did.

Finally Kimi used a riveting personal experience as her third example. It's instructive to note that this is pretty much the same paragraph she had prepared in advance while she was writing practice essays for me in my classes (For a quick look at an earlier version of this paragraph, see Chapter 7, *Details, Details, Details*). So she simply dusted off this prefabricated paragraph resident in her Bag of Tricks and applied it to the prompt at hand. The Horatio Alger aspects of her story no doubt impressed the SAT Readers.

Prompt: Is it important to question the ideas and decisions of people in positions of authority?

Conor W., October 2006 SAT (score = 12)

Musician and author Frank Zappa once wrote that "Without the questioning of authority, progress is not possible." This quote demonstrates the importance of critical analysis of authority figures in order to make better decisions based on fact and on what is the most beneficial for the people. Examples of the importance of questioning authority figures can be found in history, literature, and art.

During the Civil Rights movement of the 1980s, Reverend Martin Luther King Jr. began to lead a quest for the equality of African-American men and women. Prior to this movement, the "separate but equal" mentality of the United States had been abused in order to oppress African Americans. In Reverend King's most famous speech, "I have a dream", the Reverend spoke fiercely against the authority figures who had been conspiring against the African-American race. "You can say we have equality but instead pollute our minds with words that have no meaning. And I tell you now, I question those words and demand an explanation. I demand equality!" Reverend King's call for the people to began to think freely and question those in power became the driving force behind a peaceful revolution that was an essential step forward for African-American rights.

In Nathaniel Hawthorne's novel *The Scarlet Letter*, Hester Prynne is forced to wear a Scarlet Letter "A" as a sign of her adultery. Prynne is judged by her entire puritan community and becomes frowned upon by authority figures. However, Hester soon begins to question why *The Scarlet Letter* must symbolize "Adultery". Prynne begins to become an astonishingly helpful member of her society. Her artwork is revered by the very people who ostracized her. She also becomes a great benefactor to her community. Soon, Hester's letter "A" becomes a symbol for "Able" rather than "Adulteress". Hester's refusal to accept the biased way people saw her and her insistence on questioning those in authority leads her to become a helpful human being and an important member of the puritan community.

Another compelling illustration of the importance of questioning authority can be seen in poet and musician Tupac Shakur, whose unorthodox lyrics and anti-establishment belief system led an entire generation to begin to question what those in power were telling them. In what is arguably Shakur's most important song, Tupac writes, "I see no changes, all i see is racist faces, misplaced hate makes disgrace erase us." In this scathing attack on modern society, Shakur insists that the changes and equality promised to us all have been ignored and instead exchanged for war and injustice. Shakur's fans began to rally behind this demand. This uprising of young people became an important step towards equality.

The ability to question authority is what makes our country so diverse, however, people lose sight of this and it is important to remember to question authority in order to progress. This idea is essential to the progress of mankind. For without questioning authority, we are doomed to be oppressed for eternity.

Comments

Notice how Conor effortlessly spins the prompt to associate questioning authority with social progress. In some sense, he's banking off of a prior SAT prompt (Does progress depend on people with new ideas) to buttress his argument that questioning authority leads to social progress. It's a brilliant marriage of prompts and ideas.

Also note his use of language: "Her artwork is revered by the very people who ostracized her." And: "In this scathing attack on modern society, Shakur insists that the changes and equality promised to us all have been ignored and instead exchanged for war and injustice."

Conor also does a terrific job of remembering (or imagining!) quotes from Frank Zappa, MLK and Tupac to advance the narrative.

Great stuff, but what I *really* like about this essay is how Conor weaved the old (MLK and Hester Prynne) and the new (Frank Zappa and Tupac Shakur, the seminal rap artist of the 90s) demonstrating total command of the basic SAT template principles I taught him while bringing originality and personal insight of his own into the mix.

This is a great example of writing that both applies the basics and then supersedes them. Star pupil.

Prompt: Are people's lives determined by chance events or do individuals control their own destinies?

Nick D (practice essay)

In the novel *Gravity's Rainbow*, author Thomas Pynchon once wrote that, "This world is not a schedule so what's the point of walking in a straight line, eh?" In a rather nonchalant tone, Pynchon is essentially describing how human beings are doomed to coincidences, no matter how careful they live their lives. Even in our most simplistic plans and undertakings, we are ultimately subject to unexpected, chance events that can alter the course of our judgment and destiny. These aspects of fate can be traced throughout 20th century history into fields of science, history, as well as the arts.

One illustration of this notion can be seen in the strange 1995 David Hahn incident, in which Hahn, a 17 year old adolescent, attempted to construct a nuclear reactor in his parent's potting shed. Comprising wide knowledge of his subject as well as an idealistic perspective, Hahn set out on his work forging aliases and cover stories to retrieve materials for his project. He ended up getting significantly far into his creation, when fate managed to catch up with him when authorities barged into his shed following a police call. All his work was taken away and buried, and what could have been a brilliant scientist now resides on the U.S.S. Enterprise as a sailor, simply because of that one chance event.

Another illustration of this undercurrent of fate lies in the horrible implications of Hurricane Katrina, which devastated the city of New Orleans in 2005. In the wake of the storm, FEMA as well as the federal administration began plans to assist the stranded residents in their flooded homes with food and medical supplies. Yet, this carefully planned out process was halted by the inability to land planes or access cars to the city, and thus the once thriving city became a hellhole of violence and hunger. This well known example is another presentation that brings out the truth in Pynchon's words.

A third illustration of unexpected coincidences can also be seen in films, most especially *Dog Day Afternoon*, a 1975 film about a bank heist gone awry. Armed with machine guns, the main character Sonny played by Al Pacino storms into a bank to retrieve money for a friend's surgical operation. Yet as the hours fly by, Pacino's plan begins to disintegrate as the police surround the bank, and his composure nears its breaking point. This rather morbid example proves that chance events are part of the lives of regular people on a regular basis, no matter how ambitious the plan.

As we have seen, there is simply no schedule in life, and there are many unexpected forks in the road no matter how careful we live it. These diversions, sometimes tragic and sometimes beneficial, nevertheless prove to us that life is indeed a chameleon.

Comments

This essay is extraordinary in both its scope and depth. Not only does Nick invoke Pynchon, one of America's great esoteric novelists, to get the ball rolling, he also includes examples from eclectic sources: a bizarre, but real-life recounting of David Hahn's home-grown nuclear activities, a reference to the chaos induced and damage done by Katrina, and a colorful description of a cinema cult classic. The sheer range of examples used in this 25 minute essay is breath-taking. Well, truth be told, Nick actually took 28 minutes to write this. Even more impressive. The writing itself is sophisticated, elegant, philosophical and poignant. It doesn't get any better than this. Nick may give Pynchon a run for his money some day.

Prompt: Can books and stories about characters and events that are not real teach us anything useful?

Sarah H., November 2006 SAT (score = 11)

The famous Greek philosopher Aristotle once said, "books enlighten the mind." For all of us, the stories in books and literature are closely correlated with our own lives, even if they are fictional. As we grapple with life and our internal problems, books have the power to teach us how to overcome adversity and prejudice. This universal theme is reflected in various works of literature.

One compelling example of the idea that books can open our minds and show us how to understand humanity is shown by Khaled Hosseni's *The Kite Runner*. This story unfolds through the narrative of an Afghan boy named Amir, who is coming of age in the midst of violence and conflict within his home country. After betraying his closest friend Hassan, Amir is initially tormented by his actions but believes he can escape them by immigrating to America. However, once he has settled in his new country, Amir's memories of betrayal continue to nag him to the point where he questions the entire purpose of his life. It is not until he returns to Afghanistan that Amir is able to forgive himself by caring for Hassan's son, an act that redeems Amir from the seemingly insurmountable memories of betrayal. Throughout *The Kite Runner*, Amir shows the reader how simple acts of personal forgiveness and redemption can alter the course of one's life.

The Scarlet Letter by Nathaniel Hawthorne similarly reveals one character's personal growth in the face of adversity and prejudice. The protagonist, Hester Prynne, is forced to wear the letter A, connoting the sin of adultery, on her bosom as punishment for her illicit affair with Mr. Dimmesdale. Hester is looked down upon by Puritan society, which completely denounces her sin as an unforgivable act. Despite the circumstances, Hester overcomes this social prejudice that has defined her personal identity by reaching out to the community. By the conclusion of the novel, Hester's A has undergone a change in meaning— society no longer views it as a symbol of adultery but as a symbol of Hester's ability. This book depicts the importance of overcoming unjust prejudice that is often prevalent in today's world.

A final example of the close parallels between fictional books and real life can be seen in the novel *To Kill a Mockingbird*. Here, the town of Maycomb witnessed the racial prejudice against Tom Robinson, a black man accused of raping a white girl. The story's narrator, Scout, develops as the story progresses because she begins to recognize the prejudice and discrimination that pervades her entire town.

It is important to see that literature and books, though often fictional, are directly applicable to what goes on in our own lives. They have the power to enlighten and point out the necessity of social change.

Comments

Can you believe Sarah received an "11" on this essay instead of a perfect score? This just goes to show how unbalanced, if not outright idiotic, some of the SAT Readers can be. This is an excellent piece of writing and the fact that it didn't receive a "12" is just criminal. Look at the word choices: "enlighten, correlated, grapple, unfolds, tormented, insurmountable, redemption, connotating, illicit, denounces, depicts and pervades". Outstanding vocabulary, all in perfect service to the arguments Sarah gives in support of the prompt. Look at the sentence structure, the subordination, the transitions, the sheer intelligence and insight of the writer!

Whatever Reader gave Sarah a "5" on this essay should be taken out back, blindfolded and shot. At the very least stung by 1000 bees. Unfortunately, this kind of thing — unfair and imbecilic grading — goes on way too often in the SAT. It's like an incompetent umpire making a bad call in a championship game and the home teams suffers. Bastards. But I digress.

Another important thing I want to point out in regard to this essay is the prompt. For the first time since the essay appeared as a part of the new SAT, a prompt was provided that precluded the use of examples from history, culture, science and (aside from bedtime stories) personal experience.

Fortunately, my students, are prepared to spin the prompt and think on their feet when new ideas are tossed their way so Sarah came out swinging and hit one out of the park. But it seems to me that the College Board may be compressing the prompt to an unfair and culturally narrow focus. This is supposed to be a writing test not a *literature* test.

Prompt: Does progress depend on people with new ideas rather than on people whose ideas are based on the traditional way of doing things?

Stephanie W., May 2005 SAT (score = 12)

Our world is based on new ideas and those ideas come from individuals with vision. The common notion that progress depends on those with new ideas can be illustrated by the decline of the Native Americans and the suffrage movement of the 1900's. Humans, throughout history, have let their governments overpower and control those under its power. Whether the progress is for good or bad, that progress is provoked by people with new ideas.

Firstly, progress can surface in different circumstances. With the forced downfall of Native Americans, the white Europeans took it in their hands to continue their progression of colonizing the new world, stopping at nothing, justified by manifest destiny or God's Will. The progression of white settlement westward took on the face of genocide with the Indian Removal Act of 1830 signed into the United States 21st congress by president Andrew Jackson. The actual relocation took ten years but at the end of it, the Cherokee nation sued the United States government for the illegal advancement in progress the United States was trying to make against the Native American nation. In the court case "Cherokee Nation vs. the State of Georgia", Supreme Court justice John Marshall ruled in the Cherokee nation's favor. Nonetheless, Andrew Jackson would stop at nothing in his thirst for power, he saw the Native Americans in the way of progress and because of these fabricated ideas, all natives must be removed. He stated, "It is John Marshall's decision, now let him enforce it. "Obviously, no one could stop the president or the United States government. Like a pack of bandits, they looted the New World for everything it had to offer and so began the forced march across the great plains by the Cherokees, which became know as the "trail of tears". This journey destroyed two thirds of the Cherokee nation with hunger and disease. The indigenous people of North America were callously forced to the brink of suicide, striped of their land, culture and way of life. The policy of good faith toward Native Americans by the United States government was replaced with a policy of coercion all justified in the name of progress for the land-hungry Europeans.

Another compelling example of how progress is seen through people with new ideas is that of the suffrage movement of the early 1900's. Alice Walker was a suffragette, who organized sit-ins, peaceful protests, and hunger strikes in order to raise awareness for inequality against women. Her and thousands of other suffragettes united together to overcome the United States government. For thousands of years women were recognized as the lower of the sexes with no rights. But because of Walker's radical means and new ideas, she helped bring into passage the 19th Amendment in 1919. Progress of Woman's Rights and equality between the sexes was brought one step closer with the help of Alice Walker.

Progression, whether for the good or for the bad, is clearly exemplified through Native Americans and the suffrage movement. Both situations were inspired with people with new ideas, which is the very root of progress for our world.

Comments

Stephanie is an excellent writer who uses complex sentence structure to convey her ideas. For example: *"Like a pack of bandits, they looted the New World for everything it had to offer and so began the forced march across the great plains by the Cherokees, which became know as the 'trial of tears'."* And: *"With the forced downfall of Native Americans, the white Europeans took it in their hands to continue their progression of colonizing the new world, stopping at nothing, justified by manifest destiny or God's Will."*

But what's really interesting about this piece is the way she utilized her classroom history expertise to lend authenticity and detail to her essay. Turns out that just prior to taking the SAT, she had been working on a history term paper that dealt with 19th century treatment of Native Americans. As a result, she had a tremendous amount of detail at her fingertips that she could work into her essay.

In particular, she cites the Indian Removal Act of 1830, the "Cherokee Nation vs. the State of Georgia" court case and makes reference to the 21st congress, President Andrew Jackson and supreme court justice John Marshall. Terrific detail, impressive references. So guys, if you haven't noticed by now, you haven't been paying attention: AP history classes really pay off!

The upshot is — be sure to **dust off any term papers you've worked on** prior to taking the SAT.

Prompt: Are heroes important to modern society?

Nathan B (practice essay)

Susan Plyte once said, "Everyone needs someone to look up to." While she spoke these immortal words over a century ago, they apply to the people of today as much as they applied to those of the 19th century. Heroes are as important in modern society as they have ever been. This has been proved several times through history and film.

In the early 1930s, at the height of the Great Depression, American citizens felt lost and helpless. They desperately needed a leader who could make them feel good about their country, their future, and most importantly, themselves. Franklin Delano Roosevelt, who was elected President of the United States in 1932, was capable of doing just that, as well as providing a shining example for Americans to model themselves after. Here was a man who was crippled by polio, yet stood tall in the face of economic hardship; a man who had wealth and status, yet spent his evenings speaking over the radio to Americans across the nation; a man who had power, yet worked hard to help the common man. Roosevelt became a hero to many, and although he was not able to immediately end the Depression, he restored vitality and energy to the dwindling American spirit.

The presidency of current Head of State George W. Bush presents a stark contrast to that of Roosevelt. Whether Bush's policies and actions as president have benefited or detracted from the United States is open to debate. However, it is obvious that many people disagree with Bush's methods, and see him as a corrupt man who is incapable of being a good president. Thus, many American feel a lack of strong leadership. Unlike Roosevelt, Bush does not appeal to the vast majority of the nation, and this has led to a severe division within the American public. With no one to look up to, Americans have lost faith in their government. The lack of a hero has affected the country for the worse.

The 1994 documentary *Hoop Dreams* provides a real-life illustration of the influence heroes have on children. For ten years, the filmmakers recorded the lives of young inner-city athletes William Gates and Arthur Agee, starting when the boys were in third grade and ending with their last season as college basketball players. Throughout their careers, they looked up to Isaiah Thomas, a man who had grown up in their neighborhood and made it all the way to the NBA. Thomas gives the boys inspiration and hope that their dreams of becoming professional basketball players may come true. Although having a hero like Thomas isn't able to take the boys all the way to the NBA, he provides enough of a role model to make them try to the best of their ability, despite economic and domestic hardship.

A hero can be the most important thing in someone's life, no matter who they are. As Susan Plyte said, every person needs a role model who they can look to in times of doubt.

Comments:

Nathan's essay is marked by extraordinary use of parallel structure. For example: *Here was a man who was crippled by polio, yet stood tall in the face of economic hardship; a man who had wealth and status, yet spent his evenings speaking over the radio to Americans across the nation; a man who had power, yet worked hard to help the common man.* Also: *They desperately needed a leader who could make them feel good about their country, their future, and most importantly, themselves.*

Nathan shows his understanding of history and political science by contrasting two presidents, one whom he admires (FDR) and one whom he criticizes (George W. Bush). Notice, however, how his criticism of Bush is conveyed in a measured and responsible manner so as not to appear unduly partisan. Finally, he brings in an example from cinema, a documentary involving inner city youth. He concludes by circling back to the quote he invoked in the beginning from the mythical Susan Plyte, who, as you probably know by now, is a popular surrogate used by many of my students for quote attribution and invention.

Katrina K (practice essay)

Heroes can come in all different shapes and sizes and from all different backgrounds and cultures. In fact, anyone can qualify. According to Jackie Kennedy, "A hero is someone who never abandons his or her post to fight for others." While this may be true, a hero needn't necessarily be a soldier on the battlefield, just someone who speaks out for what is right, or picks someone up when they are down. In our constantly modernizing society, more and more true heroes are needed as role-models to counterbalance false celebrity idols, especially in regard to younger generations. However, heroes have been needed just as much in the past as they are in the present. This much is evident throughout history and literature.

In the past, many religious heroes have risen up, often combating corruption, to lead the people in a new faith. One such hero to the Catholics of Germany, and then to all of Europe, was Martin Luther. In an iniquitous scheme to drain the commoners of their pocket money, the Catholic Church in Germany started the sale of indulgences. Indulgences were essentially a "ticket" to heaven for the buyer or loved ones. Many recognized this new policy by the church as highly unjust as more and more church-goers were conned by the skilled salesman Johann Tetzel. However, no one significantly spoke up until 1517, when Martin Luther bravely nailed his now famous document "The Ninety-five Theses" to the door of the church, condemning the sale of indulgences. By acknowledging what was wrong and defending what was right, Luther became a role model for the exploited church-goers. In fact, Luther's heroic behavior caused him to lead Europe in a religious revolution which caused a break from the traditionally corrupt Catholic Church and created a new sect: Protestantism.

Literature from throughout the ages also presents many highly prized examples of heroism, including a novel by Suzanne Collins, *The Hunger Games*. In a post-apocalyptic world, Katniss, the protagonist, is a young girl fighting for the survival of her family. When her sister is chosen in a dreaded government lottery with other youths who are to battle to the death in a televised arena, Katniss volunteers to take her sister's place. Although this choice means almost certain death, Katniss proceeds with the utmost courage. Not only does Katniss save her sister, she also saves other contestants in the arena who are meant to be her competitors. By defying the government, whose plan it is to display its power by setting citizens against each other, Katniss gives the oppressed people of her country hope for better lives and courage to stand up to their autocratic government.

Whatever the circumstances or the time period, normal people who step up to become heroes have been, and always will be, assets to society. In a continually changing world where the only constant is the un-expected, the general public relishes the encouraging stories of heroes. Whether completing a minor deed or accomplishing a major feat, heroes are the people who have given others cause to look up to them and be inspired. Some such role-models have been given more publicity than others, and some have even been undeserving of their admiration, but a true hero could be living right next door.

Comments:

Katrina only employs four paragraphs in this essay (rather than the traditional five) but her introduction has such historical and cultural sweep, her content examples such extraordinary analysis and detail, her writing style such flair, and her conclusion such punch, that a reader would be out of his or her mind to give this essay anything less than a perfect 12.

By the way, I included two essays on heroes in this section since it's such a good topic to practice writing essays on. Heroic actions always involve some subset of the key points for SAT essays -- drama, conflict, obstacles met, challenges overcome and progress achieved. It's an easy topic for SAT newbies to start writing on.

Prompt: The best laid plans of mice and men often go awry

Armeen K (practice essay) --

Major Edward J. Murphy's Law states, "What can go wrong, will go wrong". This simple statement has plagued not only the common person, but even the highly educated engineers and military strategists from years past to today. While man thinks that he can plan for everything, the unexpected seems to in most cases stab man in the back right when he can't afford it. From 200 years ago to today's society, it goes without saying that man is never prepared for the unexpected. This universal notion is exemplified though history, science, and engineering.

One compelling illustration that shows how man can always expect the unexpected to occur is demonstrated in the engineering disaster of the Tacoma Narrows suspension bridge. In the windy fall month of November 1940, the Tacoma Narrows bridge started to shake and sway rapidly from side to side until it finally broke. What baffled engineers the most was that they only built the bridge four months earlier. When the engineers decided to rebuild the bridge the same way, a physics professor from Caltech pleaded with them not to. He had found out that the way the bridge was built was at fault, because the winds that hit the bridge had the same natural resonance frequencies as that of the wind, therefore whenever a wind would hit that same frequency the bridge would shake wildly again. The engineers at Tacoma Narrows felt that they had built a bridge that was stable enough to handle hundreds of thousands of cars each day, but they had not even looked at the possibility of resonance destroying their creation.

The theme that one cannot prepare for everything can be seen in the Apollo 13 mission to the moon. With an experienced crew and two flights to the moon already successfully completed, NASA felt very prepared for their third mission to the moon. All seemed well in the mission until on Day 4 during an engine pressure check, the Saturn V capsule started to leak oxygen through the vital chambers near the port side of the capsule. Faced with the loss of American astronauts and the public humiliation that NASA would receive, the mission controllers planned for numerous scenarios for bringing their boys home. Luckily, Murphy's law did not take place during the vital moon orbit necessary for achieving enough speed to get back home. When the Commission for the Investigation of the Apollo 13 Mishap released their findings, apparently, a faulty oxygen pump was installed early in the construction process of the Saturn V rocket. Even with preparedness of the engineers at Mission Control, a simple oxygen pump almost killed three astronauts and the reputation of NASA.

A final illustration of Murphy's Law takes us back two hundred years to the European campaigns of the famous French General, Napoleon Bonaparte. Napoleon had previously conquered the unbeatable Prussian Grenadiers in Germany, and marched straight through Italy and the Balkans. All that was left for the master strategist was the conquering of Russian for his continental empire. Napoleon's 500,000 man strong army, Le Grandouis Armee du Republic, was ready to charge Russia. He charged through the slavic empire easily with few casualties until the Battle of Bordino in 1807. While it was technically a victory for Napoleon, his army was short on supplies, and the devastating Russian winter was only a few weeks away. Napoleon's army rushed to Moscow to take the city and replenish their supplies, however when they got there, the Russians had decimated all the resources and supplies in their retreat to St. Petersburg. This was a total shock to Napoleon who had planned his entire campaign on the capture of Moscow before the Russians so that he would be able to return without running into the horrible cold. With empty stomach and low morale, the soldiers marched en route to Paris, only to be ambushed by Russian and Prussian soldiers from the North and West, and by the ruthless cold surrounding them on all fronts. By the time Napoleon reached the French border his troop count had fallen from 500,000 to only 10,000. While he planned and prepared to only be in Russia before the winter, the unexpected came around and literally stopped him in his tracks.

As seen through these historic and scientific examples, one can never be prepared for the unexpected. However, with proper focus and dedication, as seen with the Mission Controllers of Apollo 13, it is possible to overcome the unexpected. As British General, Alfred Montgomery stated, "You can never be too prepared, if you think you are safe, you're not, if you think you have the high ground, they will get you from even higher ground."

Comments

In this dazzling practice essay, Armeen sort of went overboard in terms of time (35+ minutes) and content, but let's cut the guy some slack; I mean, he gives a brief history of the Napoleanic wars for one thing, and an engineering overview of resonance and its effect on the Tacoma Narrows bridge for another. Way to go, Armeen.

Plus, Armeen wasn't just showing off on practice tests. Later, when he took the real SAT, he scored a perfect "12" on his essay, which just goes to show: practice makes perfect.

Prompt: Is it best to have low expectations and to set goals we are sure of achieving?

Jane I., March 2007 (score = 12)

Everyone in the world has one time or another set a goal for themselves. In life though, one must have attainable goals and not set their expectations too high for themselves. Throughout past events and experiences in one's life, one must be able to understand and know the limits within reality. This universal notion is prevalent throughout history and different sources of literature, fiction and nonfiction.

In the later 1910's women were starting to keep up the push for Woman's Rights, even though all of the men were coming back from World War I. During this era there was a new term to describe this new woman, flapper. These ladies wanted to take control and go against the grain. They didn't expect immediate respect or welcoming but with high hope they started wearing more masculine styles along with organizing sports teams and rallies. Soon enough women's activists lobbied for suffrage but slowly and surely they knew their limits and example Susan B Anthony a women's rights suffragette along with Cady B Stanton didn't give up until they fulfilled their goal.

Second, Melba B. Melba, who wrote *Warrior Don't Cry*, was one of the little rock group who helped integrate Central High School. Getting involved in this fiasco, Melba knew what to expect, no respect from whites so when white women would be nice to her, she felt so amazing. Melba knew it would take time to integrate Central High and for one thing wasn't expecting this idea of "Progressive City Little Rock" to take shape. Before she knew it one was attending classes with eight other black students and she understood the harsh treatment of her white peers just to make a difference. She wasn't expecting the reality of the past to change, just to reach her goal, attending Little Rock, to happen.

Lastly, in a fiction novel called *The Scarlet Letter* by Nathaniel Hawthorn, Hester Prynne has low expectation of her reviving her life again after committing adultery in her value filled society. She took the blame and wore the "A" proud and tall. She went about life: knowing she had sinned and didn't expect anyone to ever forgive her on the other hand Rev. Dimmesdale has too high of expectations, "A" on his chest, Dimmesdale believed his act of adultery would never be known and he could go about with the society as though nothing has happened. Dimmesdale expectations did not fit reality and his guild helped lead to his untimely demise. Although Hester had confronted her wrong and expected nothing of it, in reality forgiveness prevails. The society saw her grow and shared her secret with her. This fostered the achievement of an unforeseen goal in Hester's eyes.

This notion is relevant to everyday life for the world is filled with ambitious people. Activists, throughout historical events the Woman's Rights and Civil Rights, knew how far they could expect to push until they got what they wanted. Also, novels in the world show potential lessons of reality. We must stand back and understand our limits.

Comments

A key thing to note about this essay is its length. Clocking in at 519 words, the essay seems to have overwhelmed the Readers with sheer output. Recall that Readers are particularly impressed with word count, which is why it's always important to keep the pencil moving. Keep the pencil moving. Sometimes quantity outweighs quality in the minds of the SAT Readers.

In addition, this essay has an interesting back story: bad girl makes good. Jane wasn't able to take my SAT course but, as a friend of my daughter's, was able to secure an advance copy of the book. She read it through over a two-day period and quickly absorbed the information. Here's what she had to say in an email to me:

"Tom, your book was very helpful. It put everything into perspective and made the essay a lot easier to understand. I got an 8 on my essay the first time I took the SAT's. Then I read your book. The book was so useful for constructing my introduction and conclusion paragraphs that I didn't have the burden of worrying about extra things. Just by reading different sections of this book and applying them to my essay topic, I was able to get a 12 on my second essay!"

Prompt: Do people confuse appearances with reality?

Aliyah S (practice essay)

Despite what some might hope, appearance is often the first-noticed attribute in a person. One's appearance can define their life. As Shakespeare once wrote, "It makes him, and it mars him." One must learn to see past appearances into the greater depths of reality. This universal notion is exemplified through history and literature.

One group's fight against the judgement of appearances is clearly illustrated in The Civil Rights Movement. Dr. Martin Luther King Jr. spoke of the hope that mankind will learn to judge by character, not appearance. African Americans had been oppressed for hundreds of years, and by the point of the mid-twentieth century, they were fed up. Through countless protests, marches, and boycotts, African Americans were finally able to win equality and desegregate the South.

Another example of the influence of appearances can be seen in Hitler's rise to power. After WWI, Germany was in a poor state, and was willing to latch on to any promise of a better future. Because of his strong character and persuading oratory skills, Hitler appeared to have simply Germany's best intentions in mind. By killing off groups of people, Hitler convinced the public they were killing away their country's problems. Tragically, millions were sacrificed because of the deceptiveness of Hitler's cause.

A third illustration of the deception of appearance can be seen in Herman Mellville's classic novel, *Moby Dick*. While staying at a cheap inn, Ishmael, the protagonist of the novel, is forced to share a bed with a cannibal. Standing seven feet tall, the cannibal carries his harpoon everywhere he goes, and is covered in blue tattoos. Understandably so, Ishmael is a little apprehensive about sharing his bed with a cannibal and his spear. However, early in the novel, Ishmael is soon able to see past the appearance of this man, and develops an unbreakable friendship with him. This proves the point that it is not what is on the outside that matters, but rather what you carry in your character.

Helen Keller once said, "The best things in life cannot be seen with the eye, but rather felt with the heart." This statement holds true to this day. Appearance, though a prominent feature, does not define a person.

Comments

Two things I really like about this essay: (1) Aliyah manages to work *Moby Dick* into her essay, no mean feat; and (2) she quotes Helen Keller in her conclusion to support her view that *One must learn to see past appearances*. Who better than Helen Keller to "see" past appearances, and who better than Herman Melville to delve below the surface of things and plumb the lower depths.

Prompt: Are the needs of the individual more important than the needs of a group?

Shelby L (practice essay)

Since the dawn of civilization, men and women have participated in an everlasting attempt to improve their lives, whether in their individual or communal needs. The pursuit of self-interest will always be beneficial towards the well being of a group and vice versa because a group is composed of individuals. Ultimately, neither the individual's nor the group's needs outweigh each other but instead are equally important in the advancement of society. This universal notion is best exemplified throughout history and my personal experience.

One compelling example that an individual's needs equally benefit society as well as self-interest occurs in the fight for Women's Rights in the early 1900s. Under Woodrow Wilson's presidency, women did not have the right to vote. While many women conformed to the lives men expected them to live, women such as Susan B. Anthony and Alice Paul were determined to level the field of equality between men and women. Alice Paul founded the National Women's Party (NWP) an association demanding the passing of a national suffrage amendment. The NWP was the first organization to hold a non-violent civil disobedience campaign. On January 10, 1918, the House of Representatives passed the national suffrage amendment, but it wasn't until 1919 that Senate passed the amendment granting women the right to vote. Alice Paul's and Susan B. Anthony's courage and determination for achieving Women's Rights led to a nationwide freedom for women.

Another definitive example that individual's needs are equivalent to and can benefit the community is found in the Dred Scott versus Sandford lawsuit. Dred Scott was a slave in Missouri. In 1833 to 1834, he lived in Illinois, a free state. There he resided in an area of the Louisiana Territory where slavery was abolished by the Missouri Compromise of 1820. When he returned to Missouri, he unsuccessfully sued the state for his freedom and the Missouri Compromise was declared unconstitutional. Although his individual needs were not attained through the trial, his owner granted him freedom shortly after the trial. This case helped advance the abolition of slavery throughout the nation by questioning existing statutes and laws.

One final example of the credo that an individual's needs are equal to the group's needs can be seen in my personal experience. Last summer I participated in a teen help organization. The group of volunteers consisted of high school students, all of whom contributed to this cause for credit for community service. We received numerous calls every day from teenagers asking about dating, relationships, health and peer pressure. By the end of the summer, even though we had been driven by our need for credits, it was clear to see our time spent volunteering had been useful to those who had come to us for advice.

As can be seen through these historical examples and my personal experience, an individual's needs are equally important as those of a group. This notion is particularly relevant to our lives today, for the world is undergoing change at an alarming rate. As humankind continues to strive for self-improvement, our society will continue to be forever changing.

Comments

Shelby pulls out all the stops here to give terrific, detailed examples of Women's Rights and the Dred Scott case. Her knowledge of history is impeccable.

Also her introduction and conclusion both have tremendous sweep. For example: *Since the dawn of civilization, men and women have participated in an everlasting attempt to improve their lives, whether in their individual or communal needs.* And her conclusion: *This notion is particularly relevant to our lives today, for the world is undergoing change at an alarming rate. As humankind continues to strive for self-improvement, our society will continue to be forever changing.*

As an entrance and exit strategy, it's always a good idea to make bold, sweeping, pan-and-scan statements in your introductions and conclusions. It lets the reader know you comprehend the big picture.

Prompt: Is talking the most effective and satisfying way of communicating with others?

Shannon G, May 2010 (score = 12)

> As Albert Einstein once said, "the greatest barrier to success is fear of failure." Although this phrase may seem hackneyed in the minds of many, its authenticity is immense. Einstein demonstrated this very saying throughout all of his actions. His journey to become "one of the greatest mathematicians in history" was filled with triumphs and behind these triumphs many failures. If Einstein had talked to effectively satisfy and communicate with others, he would not have done the ground breaking things he did for fear of failure and society. This notion is exemplified throughout history, literature, and my own personal experience.
>
> Phyllis Wheatley, born in Gambia Africa in 1754, was sold at the juvenile age of seven as a slave. Brought over by ship to the US, Wheatley was purchased by Joe and Susanna Wheatley. Although her original purpose was as a slave, Phyllis Wheatley was soon integrated as part of the family and was raised along with the other children. By the age of twelve, Wheatley was able to read the Bible as well as many other Greek and Latin classics. Her true talent surfaced when she composed her first poem at the age of thirteen. Soon after, Wheatley published her first book, "A Collection of Poems: Religious and Moral" and became an instant sensation. Not only was Wheatley the first African American to publish a book, she was a woman as well. If Phyllis Wheatley had tried to talk to others, she would not have done the ground breaking things she did. Instead, she broke the bounds of her society and ignored her restraints to become an educated and well respected woman, hailed by men such as George Washington.
>
> Another prime example surfaces in John Steinbeck's migrant workers classic, *The Grapes of Wrath.* the Joad family suffers greatly throughout the story and are slandered with the name "okies." Instead of trying to communicate with others, Ma Joad acts to keep her family together. This faculty is best exemplified as the family makes its treacherous journey across the California

Desert. All the while Ma Joad suffers with the knowledge that Grandma has passed away. When confronted with the reason behind her action, Ma simply states: "the famly hadda get acrost." Ma met her challenge unflinchingly and without a word so her family could make it to California in search for a better life.

Lastly, I find in my own experiences that talking to others is not the most effective way to make a statement. When trying out for the Varsity Cheer Squad as a freshman, I was ridiculed and verbally tortured by the other girls. Instead of communication, I practiced every single day to perfect my routine. As the day of the tryouts came, I preformed my routine perfectly and made the squad. I showed all of the older girls what I was capable of and broke my own mental boundaries without communication.

Thus, talking is not the most effective and satisfying way of communicating with others as exemplified throughout history, literature, and my own personal experience. It is a persons actions that communicates a message to others and leads to the success of humanity. Each person, all the same, is capable of success if they are willing to overcome the obstacles of society and defy their own fears of failure.

Comments

This essay is particularly noteworthy for its spin. Immediately after the May 2010 SAT exam, many of my students reported back that they were initially surprised by the topic and needed a few minutes to devise their spin. Not so Shannon, who recognized immediately that all drama involves communication (or lack thereof) and reached into her Bag of Tricks for a few "hero" examples to incorporate into body paragraphs.

She uses Phyllis Wheatly's publication of a book as a provocative "communication" example, then spins *The Grapes of Wrath* in the opposite direction, citing Ma Joad's silence in the face of adversity as the most effective means of communicating preserverance to her family. Finally, in her personal experience paragraph, Shannon lets actions speak louder than words. Terrific spin.

Prompt: Is creativity needed more than ever in the world today?

Mojan A (practice essay)

"This nation will be lead not by orthodox thinkers, but rather by the creative, the innovative, and the people striving for true excellence" voiced Hillary Clinton during the recent Democratic Convention. In her national address, Clinton was explaining that progress is dependent on people with new, creative ideas, that a society can only advance when it adapts. These creative ideas depend on the sacrifice and determination to charge any obstacles by the people who put these ideas in motion. This belief is reflected in various books of modern literature.

One illustration that demonstrates the notion that creativity is necessary for progress is seen in the world renowned novel *Three Cups of Tea* by Greg Mortenson. This true story follows Mortenson around the world to a little known Pakistani village. After a failed attempt to climb K2, he is taken in by the member of this secluded village and nursed back to health. On the day of his departure, he vows to return and build a school for this impoverished community, regardless of the daunting obstacles he would have to overcome. In order to do what many before had failed to accomplish, Mortenson is forced to sacrifice all of his worldly possessions and much like the lone ranger of the modern world, it is left to him to uncover a way to raise funds. It is with his strength, determination and most importantly creative outlook the he is able to figuratively slay Goliath and build fifty-five schools in Taliban infested territory.

Another novel that strikes the core of the belief that with creativity follows progress is found in the nonfiction novel *The Freedom Writers* by Erin Gruwell and her one hundred and fifty students. This diary is about the amazing courage and determination of a teacher and her students to combat the adversity each faced day in and day out. Dubbed an "idealistic teacher", Gruwell's students, a mix of African-American, Latino, Cambodian, Vietnamese and Caucasian ethnicities, make bets on how long she will last and are determined to give her the cold shoulder. Rather than succumb to temptation and leave the gang-ridden Long Beach school as many teachers had before, she stays and begins her quest to connect with her students. She challenges her students to rethink their unyielding images of themselves and through her endeavors, Gruwell takes a class divided by gang wars and turns them into a close knit family. Erin Gruwell's is a classic American tale, a tale that proves that any obstacle can be leaped, any boundary can be broken.

These two novels support the belief that creativity is a necessary component in striving for progress. With the countless issues plaguing society today, innovative thinking and actions will be necessary to make stability a viable dream. After all, was it not John F. Kennedy who stated "The world is ours to shape, all we have to decide is how".

Comments

Using four paragraphs instead of five to get the job done, Mojan sets the scene with a quote from Hillary Clinton, then delves deeply into two strife-torn examples of courage, creativity and hope -- in short, drama -- to get her point across. Her writing style is fluid, sophisticated, and sharp. Mojan would make a great journalist for an international news organization.

≡

Golnoosh G (practice essay)

Progress, the capacity to change and improve, is a fundamental capability of mankind. Throughout the ages great thinkers have used their keen and unique intellect to promote change. This change, however, accompanies revolutionary philosophies, some that were disapproved of or deemed heretical during the time of their creation. Thus, progress is fully dependent on the creativity of certain individuals in solving everyday problems. Since the beginning of mankind, this notion intertwining progress and creativity has been prevalent.

The Industrial Revolution, the intellectual revolution that occurred during the 17th century, allowed society to make advancements impossible without the creative minds that dominated the age. New inventions and technical advances allowed industry to make changes that profited workers all over Europe. Certain individuals solved the hindrances of the age by integrating creativity with their ingenuity. For example, James Watt made the revolutionary discovery and invention of the steam engine, thus transforming European society. This one invention united the continent by providing transport through railroads and ships. James Watt changed society by using new ideas in response to common difficulties such as transport and communication. Similarly, two inventors, Richard Arkwright and James Hargreaves, brought Europe into the modern inventions with their discoveries. Arkwright's water frame and Hargreaves' spinning jenny revolutionized the textile industry which was already gripping Europe. Their inventions created more efficient methods for spinning cotton in the factory. However, their success and ability to provide Europe with such fundamental technology was a result of their uniqueness of thought in comparison to other thinkers of their age. Just as thinkers of the Industrial Revolution used creativity to bring about the progress of society, the thinkers of the Scientific Revolution did so as well.

Another historical time period which witnessed the birth of new ideas as a result of creative individuals was the 18th century Enlightenment. The Enlightenment was a broad intellectual and cultural movement that gained strength gradually until about 1750. John Locke was one enlightenment individual who managed to change society with his creativity of thought. His Second Treatise Of Civil Government set forth a new theory about how humans learn and form their ideas. He thus rejected prevailing views that humans are born with ideas, but insisted that ideas derive from experience. Locke changed the way society viewed knowledge and later education, but did so only by questioning traditional views with creative ones. Montesquieu was another philosophes, the French term for philosopher, who was extremely influential during this time period. His novel *The Spirit of Laws* was instrumental in the creation of government in America. He argued for a separation of powers in which political power be divided and shared by different classes. This structure is seen currently in today's government. Montesquieu developed his idea through study and creativity and through his breakthrough allowed society and government to become more efficient. History has constantly witnessed creativity's influence on progress.

Throughout time, brilliant individuals have challenged the norm through creativity. Such individuals, through their creativity in thought, allowed society to progress. The Enlightenment and Scientific Revolutions exemplify such creativity leading to progress. It is only natural that for years to come society will only progress as individual thought does.

Comments

Like Mojan, Golnoosh has a deeply analytical mind and an impressive grasp of historical events. Both, of course, were AP Euro students, who picked up details for their content examples in numerous classroom discussions and papers.

The fact that they were able to incorporate those examples so deftly into an SAT essay is a testament both to their hard work (they wrote several practice essays for me, continually honing their content examples) and their superb writing skills. You go, girls!

Lindsey B

The great enlightenment thinker, Voltaire, once said, "Progress is a direct product of willpower and innovative minds." Like Voltaire, philosophers in the Age of the Enlightenment shared the view that people, possessing an inventive—yet rational—mindset, could create human progress. In other words, progress is made from the experimentation and execution of new ideas. The fact that innovative ideas promote progress is evident throughout our history, in the works of Dante Alighieri, the discoveries of the Scientific Revolution, and the inventions of Thomas Edison.

Dante Alighieri's new writing style incited progress in literature. Throughout the Middle Ages, most all official documents and works of literature were written in Latin, the language adopted by the Church and known only by the highly educated. As a result, few commoners could read anything. In 1310, however, Dante Alighieri began to write the *Divine Comedy*. Alighieri called his work a "comedy" because he wrote in vernacular Italian and not the conventional Latin. As the first major piece of literature in the common Italian language, the *Divine Comedy* was a completely modern approach to writing. Sparking an era of the use of national languages and therefore revolutionizing literature, Dante Alighieri is a prime example of an individual using new techniques to promote progress.

Another example in which new ideas create progress is the Scientific Revolution. The Scientific Revolution was brought about by creative thinkers and their breakthroughs in astronomy and physics. Such contributions included Copernicus' heliocentric model of the universe, Galileo's creation of the experimental method, and Sir Isaac Newton's Law of Universal Gravitation. These findings refuted the Aristotelian view of the universe and thus defied the Church itself. Paving the way for the Age of Enlightenment and modern science, the creative minds of the Scientific Revolution were quintessential attributes to human progress and modern world views.

Technological progress was achieved by the groundbreaking inventions of Thomas Edison. One of the most prolific inventors in history, Thomas Edison's many innovations were profoundly influential to today's world. In particular, Edison's inventions, such as the phonograph and motion picture camera have contributed greatly to mass communications and telecommunications. His invention of the light bulb in the early 1880s revolutionized the uses of electricity. Many people today enjoy movies, chat on their phones, and flip on the light switch without realizing that these convenient devices are all rooted to the creativity of one man.

As Winston Churchill once declared, "Progress is always possible as long as you have originality." As proven in the historical evidence of Dante Alighieri's *Divine Comedy*, the Scientific Revolution, and the inventions of Thomas Edison, progress is fueled by new ideas and new methods. If we were forever forced to stick with traditional ideologies and unadventurous methods, we would be trapped in some Dark Age, and would have never achieved all we have in the world of today. Progress, without originality, is impossible.

Comments:

You might be wondering why I include three essays in a row here all supporting the same topic. The reason is simple: creativity is the mother of all prompts. Why? Creative individuals have to overcome obstacles to ensure success, meet challenges from tradition-bound antagonists, and achieve progress, either personal, social or both. In other words, the lives of creative individuals are replete with **DRAMA**.

Over and above all that, Lindsey is such a superb writer that I simply had to include a sample of her work. Her writing exhibits such great subordination, transitions, parallel structure and flash vocab (quintessential attributes, refuted, ideological revolutions, inflicted) that it's impossible to ignore.

Moreover, her content examples are phenomenal. Starting with Voltaire, she covers a dazzling array of influential historical figures including Dante, Copernicus, Galileo, Aristotle, Newton, Edison, and Winston Churchill. Lindsey, you rock, baby!

Prompt: Does being ethical interfere with being successful?

Vivian W, March 2009 (score = 12)

Mohandas K. Ghandi once said, "Roads to success that require demeaning and devaluing others do not actually lead you to prosperity." In other words, success is not hindered, and is often promoted by ethical and moral behavior. This hypothesis is demonstrated throughout literature and history.

The idea that progress is made by ethical individuals is exhibited in the research of yellow fever during the building of the Panama Canal in 1842. After workers had been dying at a horrifying rate from the mysterious disease, a delegation of American scientists were sent down from the Rockefeller Institute to study the disease, determine the method of transmission, and ultimately, figure out a method of prevention. Each of the scientists signed up for the trip with the understanding that it was very likely that they would die from the disease – it affected and killed over 50% of foreigners that traveled to Latin America. They put the rest of their lives aside in order to save the lives of thousands of individuals in the future. Through their conscious efforts to save lives, as well as their honest hard work, the world discovered the method of transmission of yellow fever: mosquitoes, and devised methods or prevention, effectively saving the lives of millions of individuals all over the world.

The journey of Frodo and the Fellowship of the ring exhibits the truth that even when abiding by morals and ethics, one can achieve great accomplishments. In J.R.R. Tolkien's epic trilogy, *The Lord of the Rings*, Frodo and his comrades travel vast and treacherous lands, facing goblins, orcs, and evil sorcerers, to destroy the Ring. Throughout the trip, each of the fellowship is tempted by the power of the Ring – with it, they could wage wars and win battles, effectively taking over Middle Earth and enslaving all other races, species, and clans. However, conscious of their moral duties and guidelines, each individual of the fellowship recognizes the danger and destruction that accompany the ring, and thus, reject its use for their own personal gain. In addition, the journey itself is made to save Middle Earth from Sauron and his evil minions – because of their strong moral compasses, each of the delegates of the fellowship recognize that the mission to destroy the ring is a mission that is worth the sacrifice of their own lives. The mission to restore prosperity and order to Middle Earth would not have been successful without the combined efforts of moral individuals.

Dr. Paul Farmer, the protagonist of the Pulitzer Prize-winning nonfiction account, *Mountains Beyond Mountains*, is himself the embodiment of the idea that morals and ethics are not obstacles, and may even be promoters of improvement and progress. Hardworking and resourceful, Farmer was raised in an underprivileged and impoverished family, but earned himself a full ride scholarship to Duke University. He later continued to Harvard Medical School, but instead of attending classes and burying himself in books while staying unaware of the pressing matters of the world, Farmer spent most of the semester setting up a free clinic in Haiti for desperate and destitute patients. His strong sense of right and wrong pushed him into action while other less aware students would have plodded on through their education without making a difference in the world. Farmer still graduated at the top of his class, with honors, and continued his education to receive a PhD from the University, all while saving the lives of thousands of patients.

As proved by literary and historical examples, individuals that uphold and promote morals and ethics often succeed their goals, even without the exploitation of other individuals.

Comments

It's rare for a junior in high school to have both a dazzling command of the English language AND a profound understanding of the moral complexities that motivate individuals, real and fictional. Vivian, of course, has both and weaves a compelling, extremely detailed narrative to absolutely ace her SAT essay.

Prompt: Does society benefit when individuals pursue their own goals?

Shannon B (practice essay)

William Shakespeare once said "Be not afraid of greatness. Some are born great, some achieve greatness, and some have greatness thrust upon 'em." All over the world people have overcome fears and obstacles to pursue their own goals. Not only does this pursuit benefit society, but it inspires others to be opportunists. This idea of individuals being great is exemplified throughout history and art to ensue progress in the world today.

In 1607, English settlers landed in Virginia where Indians waited to attack them. The Indians captured one of the English leaders, Captain John Smith and would have killed him, if the Indian Chief's daughter, Pocahontas had not saved him. Her desire for peace was so great that she risked her life by dramatically interposing her head between his and the war clubs of John Smith's captors, her own people. Pocahontas became an intermediary, ensuing peace between the Indians and the Settlers. However, when Lord De La Warr arrived in 1610 carrying orders to mount a war against the Indians in the Jamestown region, the Indians thought their death would be inevitable without the weapons and the tactics that the English beheld. Seven years later, the first Anglo-Powhatan War ended when a peace settlement was sealed by the marriage of Pocahontas to an English colonist John Rolfe – the first known interracial union in Virginia. Pocahontas was resolute in her goals, and was able to benefit society and become a role model for the rest of the world.

Bill Gates didn't listen to the people who told him he would be ruining his life if he dropped out of college. He kept hearing how much potential he had and he knew that he didn't want to waste years of his life in a place that bored him. He knew what people expected of him, and he knew that he didn't need to be in college to conquer that expectation. So at age 19, he dropped out of college, and created a business called Microsoft, a system that has enabled other business and people everywhere to do their jobs in an easier and faster fashion. This innovation is not only used everywhere every day, but has employed thousands of people and provided thousands of dollars of taxes. With the money he attained he set up a trust fund that will give huge sums of his money to charity when he dies. People like Gates who pursue their goals, are those who benefit society.

Finally, the photographer Ansel Adams pursued his own goals to benefit society today. Color photographs were on the rise, but Adams believed that true pictures could be beautifully taken in black and white. He took many pictures in national parks, especially in Yosemite and was not only known for these excellent pictures but also for being an environmentalist. He also created the Zone system which allows more depth and clarity in photographs by determining proper exposure and adjust the contrast of the final print. Today he is known for being one of the best black-and-white photographers and an inspiration to many.

The notion that goal setting is essential to progress in society is depicted by many people in history and art. People everywhere have overcome obstacles and met many challenges to follow their goals and to benefit society. So today, if you become frightened, instead, become inspired.

Comments

Shannon grabs the reader's attention with an opening quote from Shakespeare and then blends history, technology and art together in a brilliantly cohesive essay.

≡

Prompt: Are new ideas vital to the advancement of society ?

Audrey B (practice essay)

Imagine the world 300 years ago. There were no television, no phones, no electricity, and no cars. The majority of even the most successful explorers were convinced that the earth was flat. Now think of the world today. We have roads connecting entire countries, it is thought of as absurd if an American does not own a car, and we think it is the most ridiculous idea that the world could ever be thought of as flat. Those people that thought of the new ideas are the ones that have improved and molded the world that we know today. If they had just stuck to what they knew, the world would stay the same and not make any progress. New ideas and creativity are what helps us get around the barriers that have no obvious solutions and the problems that do not have the answers written out for us to access. The most creative figures in history, literature, and life in the world today have been some of the most successful, influential people of all time because of their ability to solve the most complicated problems with creative, new solutions.

New ideas have led to success many times throughout world history. One of the most inventive and unprecedented ideas of all time was led by Mahatma Ghandi, the man who was the face of the Indian independence movement. Like Rosa Parks, Ghandi started by refusing to give up his first class seat on a train while holding a valid first class ticket. He moved to much bigger and influential things such as speaking in conferences in World War I as a representative for the Indian people, but saying for himself that he would "personally will not kill or injure anybody, friend or foe." By remaining non-violent, Ghandi inspired many other Indians to do the same and it led to the revolution and reshaping of an entire country and its culture.

New ideas are also vital in literature; the characters who we see as the most heroic are the creative, spontaneous people. In the novel *Harry Potter* by J.K. Rowling, the protagonist, Harry Potter, is faced with all sorts of challenges at the end of each of the seven books, all involving some battle involving the darkest wizard of all time, Lord Voldemort. Harry's creative ideas are what leads him to defeat Voldemort in each book; in the second book he uses the tooth of Voldemort's monster to destroy Voldemort himself, and in the seventh novel Harry realizes that he must show the Dark Lord what he lacks compared to Harry in order to defeat him: something worth fighting for. Harry more often than not uses the less obvious strategy, his mental strength and new ideas rather than his physical strength, which leads him to kill Voldemort in the end.

Lastly, new strategies and ideas pay off in every day life. I play volleyball year-round, and to be a successful player you have to think of your own strategies. When I am trying to hit a ball straight down to the floor, but I have two 6'3 girls jumping up in front of me with their hands up trying to stuff the ball back in my face, it is very hard to avoid them. To be a successful hitter, it is your job to find a way to score points. You have to see the block and see the defenders behind it; if the right blocker isn't getting all the way out to the line, slam it off of her outside arm so the ball goes out of bounds off of her touch, if the middle back defender is stationed in the short middle of the court, tip the ball to the deep corner just out of her reach, and if the right back defender is pulling deep to dig the hard hit, tip it just over the block out of her reach. There are infinite possibilities to defeat the other team's defense, but creatively utilizing them is the hard part; but that is what distinguishes a good hitter from a great one.

In history, literature, and in every day life, new ideas trump the traditional ones in terms of success. Creativity can help one overcome all sorts of obstacles and excel in ways that others who use a mainstream and conventional approach cannot. As the creator of American Apparel, Dov Charny, once said, "the way you tell the boring people from the interesting is the creative way they present themselves and the new, fresh, and creative personalities they bring to the table".

Comments:

If you're looking for a brilliant intro to an SAT essay, it doesn't get any better than this. I love Audrey's opening line: Imagine the world 300 years ago. Talk about a grabber. In addition, her personal experience volleyball example is particularly strong, with great analysis of the game and explanation of strategic moves. Way to go, Audrey.

Prompt: Is individual achievement important to the society at large?

Stephanie P (practice essay)

Incredible individuals throughout history have shaped our world into what it is today. Like the popular adage says: "the more you believe, the more you'll achieve" it has been seen that individuals that understand and trust in themselves, are more inclined to prosper. What human nature doesn't recognize is that many times one is not able to achieve everything on his or her own. A helping hand should always be welcomed. Through pieces of literature, historical figures, and even personal experience it has been demonstrated that as humans we are not as independent as we seem and rely on others to find ourselves, and thus prosper.

In the acclaimed American classic *The Adventures of Huckleberry Finn*, Mark Twain allows the two protagonists, Huck, a young white boy, and Jim, a runaway African American slave, to create an unbreakable bond. Huck learns so much from Jim that he ultimately changes entirely as a person. At the beginning of the novel, Huck views Jim as more of a form of entertainment and a way to fill space than an actual companion. He mocks him and pulls his legs on many occasions, revealing he is as much a white bigot as the rest of society. Accustomed to conforming to society's ideals, Huck Finn breaks from this mold and eventually decides he will help free Jim from slavery. After a long fight with himself, Huck is able to realize that freeing Jim is the right thing to do and that even if he has to go to hell, he is going to do it. Jim really helps Huck see and understand that what society believes is not always correct, and that friendship is one of the most important life qualities.

Throughout history individuals such as Marcus Garvey have tried to change the world, but have realized that without the support of the people behind them their movements cannot take off. During the 1920s Marcus Garvey wished to bring African Americans to "terms" with their heritage and wanted them to believe that "black is beautiful." Garvey believed that the blacks needed to believe they had a "Homeland" in Africa and that going back to their roots would allow them to grasp themselves better. Marcus Garvey's "Back to African" movement did not take off because he did not have the support of the people behind him. In the 1920s many African Americans were having trouble respecting themselves, and they did not believe that going back to Africa was the solution to their problems. Garvey believed if people only understood why he was asking them to do this, then they would have a different mindset.

My own personal experience has shown me that I need people to understand me in order to get ahead. Although I have not done anything as noble as trying to create a movement, I have made incredible friendships. I have known one of my best friends since my freshman year of high school. When we first met we believed that we were the same person. We were so alike in many ways: we had the same taste in clothes (shared many of the same shirts), listened to the same types of music, and ate all the same foods. What we did not realize was that our personalities were quite different. Possessing the same sense of humor, we were not the same type of thinkers. She enjoys analyzing every little detail of life, while I try to be carefree and live without worries. It was and has been crucial to our friendship to understand each other and be able to identify what the other's reaction to your action will be, before even completing your action.

The Adventures of Huckleberry Finn, Marcus Garvey, and the relationship with one of my best friends are all clear examples of how it is necessary to understand other people in order to understand yourself and excel. These examples demonstrate that human nature generally progresses once understanding themselves, and being in agreement with those around them. And as Thomas Jefferson once said: "Imperative as it is to understand myself, my neighbor must be included as well."

Comments:

What I like about this essay is the psychology it brings to the SAT essay. Stephanie doesn't just "describe" actions and events, she "analyses" the underlying motivations of the individuals involved. She gives the reader an insight into the moral perspective of Huck Finn, the social and political perspective of Marcus Garvey, and her own personal perspective on the intricacies of friendship. All this accomplished with an elegant, sophisticated and polished writing style.

Prompt: Is it more important to do work that one finds fulfilling or work that pays well?

Ali K., January 2007 (score = 12)

Susan Plyte once said, "Money isn't everything. Happiness and the fulfillment that comes from staying true to yourself are the only true measures of wealth." Many people find jobs that they do not love or deem important, and their happiness is hindered in the process. Individuals who have a true impact on society, and indeed the world, have such an impact through the success of achieving what they believe is right. This universal notion, that it is far better to be fulfilled by doing what you love than to have monetary success, is exemplified throughout history, literature, and technological advancement.

One compelling illustration of the benefits of fulfilling work is demonstrated in the Civil Rights movement. Martin Luther King Jr., a brilliant and inspiring leader of non-violent protests and boycotts, did not "have a dream" that he could be wealthy. Instead, he worked incessantly for the rights of his people, despite the limited material gains his fame provided him with. Dr. King led a life that had an extremely important impact on society and on the world. Dr. King himself once stated, "We can never be truly wealthy as long as there is poverty in the world."

Another illustration that personal fulfillment is more important than money is Nathaniel Hawthorne's *The Scarlet Letter*. In this classic novel, the protagonist, Hester Prynne, is forced to wear a scarlet letter "A" upon her clothing to identify her as an adulteress. However, as Hester becomes used to her embarrassing mark of shame, she begins to help others in her community, even through her position as an outcast. Her monetary gains are extremely small, but she instead recaptures her dignity as the town people begin to refer to the "A" as meaning "Able" instead of "Adulteress". Thus, the rewards Hester gains from being a caring person and doing what is right far surpass any rewards that money might bring.

A last example that doing what you love is more important than material wealth can be seen through the technological achievements of individuals. For instance, Thomas Edison led an extremely frugal life while testing hundreds of different metals before finally discovering the practical uses of tungsten for the light bulb. Albert Einstein could barely support his family while working a long day job and philosophizing in the evenings, before finally discovering his brilliant theory of relativity. If these individuals had focused on monetary gains rather than persistence in the search for personal fulfillment, we would not have many of the practical inventions that we still use today.

While money may be emphasized in society today, the truth remains that the actions of historical leaders, fictional characters, and famous scientists brilliantly show this. As W.E.B. Du Bois stated in his autobiography, "Income is not money, it is satisfaction, it is creations, it is beauty."

Comments

Ali is a gifted writer who nailed this essay backwards and forwards. She gets off to a brilliant start by attributing a popular quote (*Money isn't everything*) to the ubiquitous Susan Plyte and uses that as a springboard to introduce her essay theme that being true to yourself is more important than achieving economic gain.

She lends authority to her thesis by concluding her paragraph on MLK with a wonderfully appropriate -- and, in fact, *real* -- quote from Dr. King that stresses social prosperity over and above individual wealth.

Her final paragraph adds an original, technological slant by introducing Edison and Einstein. Ali embroiders on Einstein's poverty to good effect, even though he had a secure, middle-class job as a Patent clerk. But hey, we've quoted Einstein many times throughout this book to the effect that imagination is more important than knowledge. Ali plays that card nicely here.

Finally, her conclusion is excellent and she employs a variation of a trick learned from Tara (see Chapter 5, *Real Essays*); that is, she uses a quote from the original prompt (not shown here) by W. E. B. Du Bois to conclude her essay with a flourish. A perfect ending to a perfect essay.

Made in the USA
San Bernardino, CA
13 April 2013